World Food
FRANCE

MARKS &
SPENCER

BEVERLY LEBLANC

World Food
FRANCE

Marks and Spencer p.l.c.

PO Box 3339

Chester CH99 9QS

www.marksandspencer.com

Created and produced by The Bridgewater Book Company Ltd.

Project Editor Emily Casey Bailey

Art Director Michael Whitehead

Photography Laurie Evans

Home Economist Annie Rigg

Location photography Kim Sayer (12, 16, 61, 90, 120, 133, 160,
184, 190, 207, 220, 225), Caroline Jones (15, 19, 20, 22, 24, 33,
56, 100, 153, 205, 237, 238)

Front cover photography Mike Hemsley at WG Photo

ISBN: 1-84461-265-1

Printed in China

NOTES FOR THE READER

- This book uses both metric and imperial measurements. Follow
  the same units of measurement throughout; do not mix metric
  and imperial.

- All spoon measurements are level: teaspoons are assumed to be
  5 ml, and tablespoons are assumed to be 15 ml.

- Unless otherwise stated, milk is assumed to be full fat, eggs and
  individual vegetables such as potatoes are medium, and pepper
  is freshly ground black pepper.

- Recipes using raw or very lightly cooked eggs should be avoided
  by infants, the elderly, pregnant women, convalescents, and
  anyone suffering from an illness.

- The times given are an approximate guide only. Preparation times
  differ according to the techniques used by different people and
  the cooking times may also vary from those given.

contents

INTRODUCTION

It might sound like a cliché, but whereas many people around the world simply eat to live, the French, it can be said, live to eat. The acts of buying, preparing, cooking and consuming food are integral parts of everyday French life and for many French people mealtimes represent one of life's greatest pleasures. French chefs with a galaxy of Michelin stars take on the status of celebrity usually reserved for actors in other countries.

Centuries of rituals and traditions meet in French food culture. Children are taught from an early age, at home and at school, to look, smell and taste and then be discerning and appreciative at the table. This continues into adulthood as professional and home cooks put great importance on using the best of seasonal ingredients in their cooking. It is the daily use of local, fresh ingredients that sums up the essence of cooking in this large country.

The land of plenty

The almost perfect combination of French food and wine owes much to the country's varied landscapes, with its soaring mountain ranges, wide rivers, fertile plains and farmlands and long coastlines. As western Europe's largest country, France's 551,000 sq km/213,000 sq miles stretch from the English Channel in the north southwards to the Mediterranean, with Spain and Andorra bordering it in the southwest, Belgium and Luxembourg to the northeast and Germany, Switzerland and Italy to the east and southeast. The Atlantic Ocean provides the picturesque, rugged coastline along the west.

Agriculture is a major industry in France, making the country self-sufficient in most essential produce. France is the European Union's largest agricultural exporter and its wheat, barley, potato, sugar beet and wine harvests, seafood and food processing contribute greatly to the national coffers. France's plentiful vineyards and fertile farmlands are fed by four major rivers. The Loire flows from the mountains of the Auvergne to the Atlantic coast; the Seine from Burgundy through Paris to the English Channel; the Garonne gushes down the Pyrenees to meet the Dordogne at Bordeaux; and the powerful Rhône travels from the Swiss Alps southwards, via Lyon, into the Mediterranean. The mighty mountain ranges – whose slopes provide the perfect grazing conditions for the cows and goats that supply the dairy industry – are the Alps, the Jura and the Pyrenees. The extinct volcanoes of Auvergne also provide summer grazing lands for cows that produce some of the country's best-loved cheeses.

Many restaurateurs, chefs, farmers and diners in the 22 administrative regions that make up mainland France and Corsica do their best to resist the universal trend towards homogenization and, fortunately for visitors, regional culinary characteristics and flavours are easy to spot on menus. A never-failing rule of thumb for dining well when travelling through France is to drink the local wine with the local food.

Paris

Paris – rivalled by Lyon for the title of food capital of France – doesn't have a distinct culinary style of its own. And this is precisely why the 'City of Lights' is

the ideal starting place for a French culinary tour.
A stroll through any Parisian neighbourhood offers a
telescopic look at the traditions, sights and smells of
French cooking that are simultaneously occurring all
over the country as domestic and professional cooks
go through their daily rituals in search of the best:
the unmistakable butter-rich smells coming from the
bakeries, the strong farmhouse aromas from cheese
shops, the inviting scent of chicken roasting on
rotisseries, fresh oysters and shellfish being prepared
outside brasseries, uniformed waiters serving café
pavement tables and chairs and shoppers returning
from local markets with their full trolleys on wheels.

For an overview of the best food and wine France
has to offer, taste and shop at the food halls in the

*Paris, one of the food capitals of the world, offers a galaxy
of gastronomic experiences for the visitor to savour*

large department stores (*les grands magasins*).
Or sample a typical French market at Rue Mouffetard,
in the fifth arrondissement, with shops and stalls
lining both sides of the winding cobbled street. This
colourful, noisy market has catered for Parisians since
the fourteenth century. For an equally authentic, but
less crowded market, head for Rue Cler in the shadow
of the Eiffel Tower in the refined seventh
arrondissement. The prices are higher, but with
many Americans living nearby, language is less of a
problem. Parisian food shopkeepers, like shopkeepers
across the country, take great care preparing their

visually exciting, mouthwatering window displays. Looking and smelling are as much a part of the French culinary experience as eating.

Dining out is a regular part of French life, but nowhere else in the country is it possible to sample such a variety of regional and foreign cuisines as in Paris. Parisians are spoilt for choice when it comes to choosing restaurants for any occasion and in any price bracket. At the peak of the restaurant pecking order, Michelin-starred establishments serve sophisticated *haute cuisine*, which comes with the world's most professional waiters and some of the most expensive menus. Smaller, cosy neighbourhood restaurants bridge the gap with the more modest bistros, wine bars and cheap cafés. Along with *à la carte* menus, most restaurants offer a three- or

four-course menu for a set price (*menu à prix fixe*), many including an aperitif and half-bottle of wine per person. Small restaurants and bistros tend to specialize in *cuisine bourgeoise*, or the type of home-cooking enjoyed all over the country, such as most of the recipes in this book. To sample food from a celebrity chef without paying top prices, look for the bistros that Michelin-starred chefs turn over to young protégés.

Large, bustling brasseries serve meals and drinks all day long and into the early hours of the next morning and are usually pretty relaxed. It is acceptable to order one course or an appetizer when several days of non-stop dining become overwhelming. The word 'brasserie' means 'brewery', and these big restaurants originated in Alsace,

where some of France's best-loved beers are brewed.
Enjoy a typically French experience of an espresso
at one of the tables outside a brasserie and watch
the world pass by. For a taste of typically Parisian
food, try Les Halles Onion Soup (see page 37),
Croque Monsieur (see page 70) or anything on a
menu listed as *à la parisienne*, indicating that the
dish will be garnished with small sautéed potato
balls rolled in parsley.

Northern France

The Ile-de-France, an 80-km/50-mile ring of
farmlands and forests around Paris, is where market
farmers once farmed all the produce for Les Halles,
Paris's former wholesale market that has now moved
to suburban Rungis. Some farmlands have

*The orchards of rural France produce wonderful blossoms
in the spring, later yielding an abundance of fruit*

disappeared with urbanization, but many towns
and villages are still associated with quality produce,
such as cream from Chantilly and cherries from
Montmorency. Button mushrooms are called
champignons de Paris because they were once
exclusively grown around Paris for Paris markets.

The windswept flatlands of northern France are
suited to growing wheat and corn, along with
beetroot, carrots, chicory, leeks, peas and potatoes,
which find their way into large tureens of vegetable
soup called *hochepots*. Many of the pâtés and other
charcuterie that the world enjoys as 'typically French'
come from large factories in Lille. Frog's legs are mostly

Burgundian cuisine is built around its world-class red and white wines – even the eggs are poached in wine

imported now, but frogs have traditionally been bred along the River Somme, while the baby vegetables that grace expensive restaurant meals are grown in the watery *hortillonnage* gardens around Amiens.

Flanders and Ardennes in northern France share culinary traditions with neighbouring Belgium, such as their *waterzooi*, a freshwater fish or chicken soup with local vegetables, and serving fried potatoes, or French fries, with many meals. Rabbit with Prunes (see page 98) comes from here. Leeks are big business in Picardie and the local speciality, a hot leek tart (*flamiche aux poireaux*) appears on many menus, rivalling the quiche Lorraine from its eastern neighbour. Leek and Goat's Cheese Crêpes (see page 58) and Braised Chicory (see page 195) both contain northern flavours.

The coastal ports of Calais and Boulogne attract British day-trippers for seafood lunches, but all along the northern coast fresh seafood and shellfish are a treat. Markets sell sole, cod, ling, mussels and herring, along with shellfish of every shape and colour. Jars of fish soup for souvenirs are sold in all supermarkets.

For a thirst-quenching detour, Reims and Epernay, the centres of the famed Champagne-producing region, are less than 160 km/100 miles east of Paris. All the great Champagne houses (*grandes marques*) and many less well-known ones offer cellar tours with tastings. *A la champenoise* is the local cooking style, but don't expect dishes cooked with vintage Champagne – that is reserved for celebratory toasts. Instead, bottles of still wine are used in the kitchen. Brie, the round, flat disc of cow's milk cheese that has a place on all cheeseboards, comes from the Champagne region, with the best known from Meaux.

Eastern France

Alsace and Lorraine have both been part of Germany at various times and the blend of cultures is evident in the Germanic-style cuisine, which includes salted, smoked and fresh pork, game, cabbage and many baked specialities, such as *kugelhopf*, a yeasted cake baked in a distinctive mould, and pretzels. Strasbourg ranks with Paris and Lyon as a culinary centre. Pigs reign supreme here and Alsace Sauerkraut with Pork and Sausages (see page 122), known as *choucroute*, is the culinary crown jewel. Creamy, pungent Munster cheese is served at the end of meals sprinkled with cumin seeds, recognized for centuries for their digestive qualities. Quiche Lorraine Tartlets (see page 67) are mini versions of a simple, rich tart that has travelled the world, while Tarts Flambé (see page 63) is the local version of pizza. Riesling wine is a good match for the rich food, but try *crémant,* the local sparkling wine, for an aperitif.

Burgundian cuisine is built around its world-class red and white wines, even the eggs are poached in red wine. Beef Bourguignon (see page 108) is the best-known French stew, but other local specialities include Coq au Vin (see page 78), Ham and Parsley Terrine (see page 53) and Kidneys in Mustard Sauce (see page 115). Two not-to-be-missed regional treats are the Bresse corn-fed chickens and Charolais beef. Any visit to Dijon must include a taste of mustard, *pain d'épices* (a dense, golden gingerbread) and a sip of *crème de cassis* (blackcurrant liqueur).

For gourmets and wine connoisseurs, drives along the N74 or the more leisurely D122 (*Route des Grands Crus*) pass through some of the best-known locations associated with wine production along the Côte de Nuits in the north and the Côte de Beaune. Stop and enjoy tastings at Nuits-St-Georges,

The northeastern region of Lorraine has given France its most famous flan – Quiche Lorraine

Aloxe-Corton, Beaune, Pommard, Meursault and Puligny-Montrachet, to name a few. Restaurants along the way provide what many consider the best food in France, while cheeses are available for sampling at farm gates.

Rich dishes cooked with cheese are one of the defining characteristics of the cuisine of the lush, grass-covered slopes of eastern France's dairy country. The long list of coveted regional cheeses include Beaufort, Gruyère, Tomme de Savoie, Comté and Vacherin, so rich it is eaten with a spoon. Creamy fondues are popular and Baked Vacherin (see page 68) is a quick alternative to the traditional fondue. But this region's culinary claim to fame has to be the Potato and Cheese Gratin (see page 192), the king of France's myriad vegetable gratins. It combines potatoes and Gruyère cheese with cream and garlic, a popular flavour combination. Walnut groves near Grenoble produce the oil that dresses salads all over

France, while the region also supplies the rest of the country with smoked meats and wild mushrooms.

Lyon, on the mighty Rhône river, rivals Paris as France's gastronomic capital, both in the quality of its food and the number of restaurants, ranging from Michelin-starred establishments to *bouchons*, once working-class cafés, many of which female chefs preside over. Local dishes come with the tag *à la lyonnaise*, an indication that they include onions, grown in abundance here. Potatoes and Onions (see page 194) is a typical example. Sausages, tripe and pike quenelles (*quenelles de brochet*) are specialities. The fertile Rhône Valley, following the river southwards from Lyon towards Provence, has been producing wines since Roman times. Today some of France's most popular red wines come from here – Hermitage, Châteauneuf-du-Pape and Côtes du Rhône, for example. The valley also supplies fruit bowls throughout France.

Southern and Southwestern France

For many food lovers, sunny southern France is a little bit of heaven on earth – at least in the summer when the sun warms the countryside, the Mediterranean Sea is a sparkling azure and wild herbs scent the rugged, forested inland mountains. In the winter, however, with the chilling wind, *le mistral*, blowing down from the Alps, warming dishes like Beef Stew with Olives (see page 112) are appreciated.

Garlic, olives and tomatoes flavour Mediterranean cooking – along with an abundant daily catch of seafood. Local seafood markets are fascinating and always worth a visit. Tapenade (see page 60), Ratatouille (see page 180), Scallops with Breadcrumbs and Parsley (see page 170) and Creamed Salt Cod (see page 153) are typical Provençale dishes. But the best-known speciality is bouillabaisse, an elaborate seafood soup that contains the best of the morning's

The sun spotlights one of the many isolated medieval villages that dot the rugged hilltops of southern France

catch – John Dory, eel, red mullet, perch, spiny lobster and *rascasse* (difficult to buy outside France) – in a saffron-and-garlic tomato broth. It is served with a chilli-flavoured mayonnaise (*rouille*) spread on toasted croûtes. Try Marseille-style Fish Stew (see page 162) with fennel and pastis, the local aniseed-flavoured spirit, for a much easier – and less expensive – version with all the flavours of Provence.

The Camargue, the southern land of cowboys and bulls where the Rhône reaches the Med, is known for its chewy and nutty-flavoured red rice. Garlic continues to flavour food westwards into Languedoc-Roussillon and on to Gascony. These are regions of rich food from both sea and land, of which Cassoulet (see page 129) has international fame. Its ingredients vary, but the filling casserole always contains white beans

18

Food from the Basque Country is robustly flavoured and has more in common with neighbouring Spain

and preserved goose or duck. Sautéed food takes on extra flavour here as goose fat replaces olive oil and ultra-rich goose liver, *foie gras*, is served as a first course or incorporated into other dishes. Warm salads (*salades tièdes*), popular bistro fare, are traditional. The pig is all important and sausages, hams and pâtés from around Toulouse are shipped throughout France. Blue-cheese connoisseurs flock to Roquefort-sur-Soulzon in Languedoc, where one of the most famous cheeses in the world is made from raw sheep's milk. For strictly regional delicacies, try the candied violets and violet-flavoured liqueur made near Perpignan.

Food from the Basque Country is robustly flavoured and has more in common with neighbouring Spain than the rest of France. Red and green peppers and tomatoes are the prime ingredients of regional cooking, with the occasional hint of chilli. Basque-style Cod (see page 154) is a typical dish, as is *piperade* (eggs with peppers). A good salt-cured ham (*jambon de Bayonne*) is produced here.

Western France

Norman cooks have a fantastic selection of fresh local fish and shellfish to choose from, but Normandy is best known for its apple and pear orchards and dairy farms. Most of France's butter, cream, cheese and related products, such as crème fraîche and fromage frais, come from here. Normandy's best-known cheese is Camembert, now copied all over the country, so look for cheeses labelled as '*Camembert de Normandie*'. The other great regional cheeses are Pont l'Evêque and Livarot. Apple and pear orchards fill the countryside. The fruit is used in sweet and savoury

dishes, as well as being made into cider, Calvados (apple brandy) and pear eau de vie. Any dish described as *à la Normande*, such as Pork Chops with Calvados and Apples (see page 124) and Mussels in Cider (see page 144), will contain cream along with one of the alcoholic drinks. Trout with Mussels and Prawns (see page 156) is from Dieppe. Search out lamb that has grazed on salt marshes for an authentic taste of Normandy in Roast Lamb with Beans (see page 117) or try a chicken from the Auge Valley. For dessert, make Apple Tart (see page 228) with an attractive sliced apple top.

Inland from the rugged Brittany coast, artichokes fill hectares and hectares of fields. The pink onions that grow around Roscoff are plaited and used as kitchen decorations and added to fish stews. Bretons are also known for their skill at making savoury buckwheat crêpes called *galettes* that are topped with anything from ham and cheese to prawns in a creamy béchamel sauce.

Travelling south along the spectacular Atlantic coast, a stop in La Rochelle is rewarded with fine seafood restaurants, as well as meat dishes with red wine sauces (*sauce bordelaise*), an indication that the famed Bordeaux wine estates are approaching. The red Bordeaux wines, known as clarets in Britain, are revered for their sophisticated elegance and the refined cooking of the region makes a fine match. Food here is true to its regional heritage: beef, chicken, eggs and vegetables are served *à la bordelaise*, and garlic is a popular flavouring. Cognac, the amber-coloured brandy, is produced here, as is Pineau des Charentes, a sweet blend of Cognac and grape juice most often served with foie gras.

Brittany boasts a rich diversity of fish and shellfish caught off its picturesque coastline

Overleaf Immaculate presentation is a feature of French provincial homes, where cooking is also an art form

Central France

Turreted, fairy-tale chateaux are the tourist poster image of the valley along France's longest river, flowing into the Bay of Biscay at Nantes on the Brittany coast. Known as 'the garden of France', the Loire Valley provides many of France's best fruit and vegetables and is another fine wine region, with flinty soil giving Pouilly-Fumé its distinctive taste. Sancerre, Muscadet and Vouvray wines also come from along the Loire.

Plump white asparagus is a spring treat and button-mushroom cultivation has moved here from the Ile-de-France. Loire fruit is used in sweet and savoury dishes, such as Pork with Prunes (see page 127). Orléans is known for its fine vinegars and saffron grows near Pithiviers. Freshwater fish is popular all along the Loire, often served with a rich butter sauce (*beurre blanc*).

Food from the rugged Auvergne, located on the elevated Massif Central, reflects the rural lifestyle, with cabbages and mountain pork in many guises, such as Auvergne ham (*jambon d'Auvergne*), which is salt-cured and smoked. Auvergne is also home to puy lentils, and Puy Lentils with Sausages (see page 130) is a typical rustic dish from the region. Hearty soups, such as those made with Cantal cheese, and potato dishes, such as one fried with bacon and cheese (*truffade*), are also typical. Two popular cheeses include Bleu d'Auvergne and Tomme.

Mention Limousin to anyone and the dessert Cherry Clafoutis (see page 233) comes to mind almost instantly, but this region is also known for its game dishes, with hare being popular. Many beef dishes also feature on menus.

Périgord (known to the British as the Dordogne) is home to fattened goose liver, France's most controversial gourmet delicacy, wild mushrooms

France's great rivers, as well as its seas, yield a catch of culinary delights in the shadows of the grandest chateaux

Unlike in many other countries, small traditional specialist food shops co-exist alongside the largest chains

and expensive black truffles, which pigs sniff out in forests and whose earthy flavour is added to eggs, chicken and sauces. Charcuteries provide goose and duck confit and boned and stuffed poultry dishes called *galantines* (ready to eat cold) and *ballotines* (to be cooked), ready for slicing and serving. Goose fat is used in cooking and nut oil flavours salads. A popular flavour combination is to soak prunes from Agen in Armagnac, the local brandy.

Going to market

Food shopping in France can be an absolute joy. Of course, enormous supermarkets (*supermarchés*) thrive and offer convenient one-stop shopping. Yet, unlike in many other countries, small, traditional specialist food shops co-exist alongside the largest chains (*hypermarchés*). Even the smallest village is still likely to support a bakery (*boulangerie*) for daily loaves and flaky, buttery croissants and a butcher (*boucherie*) selling fresh beef, lamb, veal, pork and chickens. If the villagers are particularly fortunate, there will also be a pork butcher (*charcuterie*), much like a delicatessen in other countries, which sells pork products ranging from fresh, cured and smoked sausages to pâtés and terrines, along with sliced cooked meats and occasionally prepared salads. It is the ideal place to buy for an impromptu picnic on a day's travels.

Other French shops include fishmongers (*poissonniers*), specialist poultry butchers (*marchands de volailles*) and butchers selling horse meat (*boucheries chevalines*). For the best of seasonal produce, go to the greengrocer (*marchand de fruit et légumes*). And, of course, as a meal in France without

wine is like a night without stars, one of the most important shops in any neighbourhood is the wine shop (*caviste*). The choice is likely to be regional, except in the larger cities, but will provide a good introduction to what is available from the most basic *vin de table* or *vin ordinaire* up the quality scale to *Vin de Pays*, *Vin Délimité de Qualité Supérieure* (*VDQS*) and *Appellation d'Origine Contrôlée* (*AOC*), which is usually the best.

Larger towns and cities have an even greater supply of shops catering for the demanding home cook. Cheese shops (*crèmeries*) sell locally produced cheese, but in larger cities the selection will expand to include the best from around the country – and what a flavoursome and varied selection it is. Indeed, General Charles de Gaulle once famously asked,

'How can you govern a country that has 246 varieties of cheese?' Savvy shoppers always taste before buying, so ask for '*une dégustation*'.

And anyone with a sweet tooth won't want to miss the mouthwatering pastry shops (*pâtisseries*), chocolate shops (*chocolateries*) or sweet shops (*confiseries*), with their tempting window displays.

Takeaway pizzas and fast-food burgers aren't yet a common feature of French life, and with good reason. When one is hungry, but not in the mood to cook, the local *traiteur* solves the problem. These are like gourmet food shops with prepared fresh meals for taking home and reheating – everything from casseroles and puff pastry vol-au-vents with creamy seafood fillings to fresh salads and snacks. Recent Chinese and Vietnamese immigrants have opened

traiteurs alongside the more traditional French ones for even more variety. *Traiteur* quality is so good that busy hosts or hostesses never have any qualms about buying one or more courses when entertaining.

Even French supermarkets have their good points. Other than in the major cities, such as Paris, Lyon and Marseille, sourcing foreign ingredients for adventurous French cooks would be difficult if it weren't for supermarkets. Busy home cooks also take advantage of frozen-food supermarkets, which sell some restaurant-quality dishes to reheat.

In a country where the demand for good quality seems insatiable, it shouldn't be a surprise that the established tradition of market shopping doesn't appear in any danger of dying out. Covered markets (*marchés couverts*) and open-air markets (*marchés*

The Château de Chambord in the Loire Valley is remarkable for the flamboyance of its architecture and its 440 rooms

en plein air) continue to thrive. In Paris, a city with an uncountable number of quality food shops, the city government regulates almost 60 markets a week, which move from neighbourhood to neighbourhood.

Provincial towns are often served by covered markets open six days a week with regular stallholders, while more rural communities rely on travelling markets that come to town one or several days a week. A good example, taken from Provence, is the charming market in Saint-Rémy-de-Provence, which is held twice-weekly. It winds its way through the narrow streets, offering everything a cook could wish for – from pots and pans to half a goat.

In the French kitchen

Bouquet garni (bouquet garni) A bundle of fresh herbs tied together and used to add flavour to liquids while they cook. A bouquet garni is discarded before serving.

To make a bouquet garni, tie one sprig of fresh thyme, two sprigs of fresh flat-leaf parsley and one bay leaf together with kitchen string. Use a long piece of string and tie the opposite end to the pan or casserole's handle, so the bouquet garni dangles in the hot liquid but is easy to remove.

Bread (pain) Few people think of French bread without thinking of the thin French *baguette* (see French Bread, opposite), but French bakers supply a variety of other loaves. Try country-style (*pain de campagne*), natural sourdough (*au levain*), organic (*biologique or bio*), walnut (*aux noix*), white sandwich loaf (*de mie*), wholewheat (*complet*), wholewheat or rye with raisins (*aux raisins*) and baked in a wood-fired oven (*pain cuit au feu de bois*). For the best loaves, look for bakeries with a sign proclaiming '*boulangerie artisanale*'.

Butter (beurre) Most French butter is unsalted and produced in Normandy and Poitou-Charentes along the Atlantic coast. Lightly salted butter (*demi-sel*) comes from Brittany and is primarily used on the table rather than in cooking. For a taste of the best from Charentes, look in delicatessens and gourmet food shops for butter labelled as '*beurre d'Echiré*' or '*beurre de Ligueil*'. Butter is the main cooking fat in northern France, while in the south olive oil is more frequently used. In the southwest goose fat replaces butter. The French rarely eat bread with butter, so if you would like some it is usually necessary to request a pot of butter in restaurants.

Clarified butter (beurre clarifié) This bright golden-yellow butter, with salts, water, milk, whey and other impurities removed, performs several functions in French kitchens. It can be heated to a higher temperature than ordinary butter without burning, which makes it ideal for sauté recipes that cook over a high heat, such as Sautéed Potatoes (see page 183). And, as clarified butter doesn't spoil as quickly as ordinary, it can also be melted and used to 'seal' pâtés and terrines. The downside of using clarified butter, however, is that when the butterfat is removed, most of the flavour is lost. That is why many recipes in this book sauté ingredients in a mixture of butter and sunflower oil, a combination that is unlikely to burn, while retaining a butter flavour.

To make clarified butter, melt butter in a saucepan of boiling water, then leave to cool completely and chill until set. The bright-yellow clarified butter can then be lifted off and melted to use, with all the impurities left behind. Alternatively, slowly melt butter in a wide saucepan and use a large metal spoon to skim off the foam. Carefully pour off the liquid, leaving any impurities on the bottom behind.

Confit (confit) Piece of goose (*d'oie*) or duck (*de canard*) slowly cooked and preserved in its own fat. A speciality of the southwest, confit is essential in most recipes for Cassoulet (see page 129). Confit is expensive, making it a good buy in French supermarkets.

Crème fraîche (crème fraîche) A thick, full-fat cream that adds a refreshing sour tang to food. It can be stirred into cooked dishes or served *au naturel* to counter the richness of desserts, such as Chocolate Tartlets (see page 226). Crème fraîche used to be made at home, but it is now widely available in supermarkets. The best quality cream reputedly comes from Isigny in Normandy.

Croûtes (croûtes) Croûtes translates as 'small pieces of toast', although occasionally some are fried (see opposite). Toasted croûtes are served topped with savoury spreads to nibble with drinks (like Italian bruschetta) or fried for a traditional garnish to stews. Clever cooks make croûtes with day-old French bread that has dried out.

To make croûtes, use 2 slices of French bread about 1 cm/½ inch thick per serving. Preheat the grill to high. Place the bread slices on a grill rack, brush lightly with olive oil and toast until golden and crisp. Turn over and repeat on the other side. Garlic-lovers can rub just-toasted croûtes with a garlic clove. Store the croûtes in an airtight container if not using at once.

To make fried croûtes, heat 2 tablespoons of sunflower oil in a large sauté or frying pan over a medium-high heat. Cut three slices of crustless bread into triangles and fry until golden brown and crisp on both sides. Drain well on kitchen paper.

Croûtons (croûtons) Fried small cubes of bread that add crunch and flavour to salads or creamy soups.

To make croûtons, pan-fry 1-cm/½-inch crustless bread cubes in a thin layer of hot sunflower oil in a sauté or frying pan over a medium-high heat, tossing and turning the cubes frequently until crisp and golden on all sides. Drain well on kitchen paper, then cool and store in an airtight container if not using at once.

Fines herbes (fines herbes) A mixture of fresh chervil, chives, flat-leaf parsley and tarragon that often flavours egg dishes such as omelettes. Packets of dried *fines herbes* are sold in French supermarkets.

French bread (baguette) The long, thin bread most French people buy fresh daily. The traditional recipe doesn't contain any fat, so the crumb becomes stale within a day. A good-quality baguette has a thin, crisp crust that makes a crunchy noise when broken. The word '*baguette*' translates as 'wand' or 'stick', the loaf's shape.

Garlic (ail) An unmistakable flavour of southern French cooking. Provençal garlic generally has smaller cloves than that grown in the Rhône Valley. Garlic is the essential ingredient of Aïoli (see page 241).

Herbes de Provence (herbes de Provence) A mixture of dried marjoram, oregano, thyme and summer savory, herbs that grow wild in Provence and flavour regional dishes.

Lardons (lardons) Pieces of bacon. Traditionally smoked pork belly cut into thin strips, although now smoked and unsmoked lardons are sold in supermarkets. Smoked lardons are often blanched in boiling water to remove excessive saltiness.

Quatre épices (quatre épices) A mix of ground cloves, ginger, nutmeg and white pepper. Sold in French supermarkets and gourmet food shops.

Sausage, dried or cured (saucisson) Ready-to-eat sausages, such as salamis.

Sausage, fresh (saucisse) Fresh sausages that must be boiled or grilled before eating. See Puy Lentils with Sausages (see page 130) for a list of popular varieties.

Stock (fond) Subtly flavoured liquid that adds taste and body to soups, casseroles, stews and some sautéed recipes. Home-made Stocks (see page 252) are superior to those made from a cube, while supermarkets sell fresh stock, which is suitable for the recipes in this book.

Vanilla Sugar (sucre vanillé) French bakers often use this fragrant sugar to add a vanilla flavour to desserts. It is sold in supermarkets and delicatessens, but to make at home leave a split vanilla bean in a sealed jar of 250 g/9 oz caster sugar for at least one week.

French cooking

Cooking *à la francaise*, or 'in the French style', has an air of sophistication and can appear difficult because of the French terms used in recipe instructions. In fact, once the terms and techniques are understood, French cooking is straightforward. The most important thing to remember is to use fresh, good-quality ingredients.

Bain-marie (bain-marie) The French term translates literally as 'Mary's bath', named after an Italian alchemist called Maria di Cleofa who 'discovered' this method of cooking, but it is commonly known as a 'water bath'. The dish to be cooked in the oven is placed in a larger container, such as a roasting tin, with boiling water coming halfway up the dish. This technique of cooking with indirect heat protects delicate dishes such as Crème Caramel (see page 209) or helps avoid overcooking dense dishes such as Country-style Terrine (see page 54).

Beurre manié (beurre manié) Equal parts of soft butter and plain flour are kneaded ('*manié*' is the French word for kneaded) into a paste, then whisked into a simmering cooking liquid to thicken the sauce. Add the beurre manié in small portions, whisking constantly, and boil after incorporation to remove the raw flour taste.

Deglaze (déglacer) To dissolve the sediment from the base of a cooking pan by adding liquid and boiling while stirring constantly. This produces a flavoursome base for sauces and gravies. The liquid used can be cream, stock, wine or even water, or a combination. A wooden spoon or spatula is the best tool for the job.

Emulsion (émulsion) The combination of two, usually incompatible, ingredients – oil and vinegar, for example – that are made smooth by beating while slowly adding one to another so that they are held in suspension. This is the basis for making a Vinaigrette (see page 244), the basic French salad dressing, and Mayonnaise (see page 241).

Flambé (flamber) Setting alight food drenched with a spirit or liqueur to burn off the alcohol, leaving behind the flavour. This technique is often employed for a tableside show in restaurants when making Crêpes Suzette (see page 219), for example. Brandy is commonly used for flambéeing, but pastis, Grand Marnier and Cointreau also feature in recipes.

To flambé a dish, heat the spirit or liqueur in a ladle over a gas flame or in a small saucepan over a medium-high heat until hot, but not boiling. Use a taper to light the spirit or liqueur and stand well back as it will dramatically burst into a bright-blue flame. Remove the saucepan with the ingredients to be flambéed from the heat, then pour over the flames and leave them to die out. Return the saucepan to the heat and continue with the recipe.

In the style of (à la) A frequently used term in French recipe titles that often indicates the regional source or style of the dish. A dish from Normandy, usually with cream and apple, is '*à la Normande*'. 'In the old style' is '*à l'ancienne*', while '*à la bordelaise*' indicates a dish from Bordeaux with red wine and shallots. '*A la Périgueux*' is a dish with truffles.

Sauté (sauter) To quickly fry ingredients – game, meat, poultry, seafood or vegetables – in a small amount of fat over a high heat. The French word '*sauter*' translates as 'to jump', so the pan should be constantly shaken to move the ingredients about. The fat, be it butter, animal fat or vegetable oil, prevents the ingredients from sticking to the pan and crisps any coating to make a thin 'crust' on the cut edges.

Moulin = windmill = fine flour = wonderful French bread!

SOUPS &
STARTERS

32 It is somewhat ironic that the French have given the world Croque Monsieur (see page 70), the toasted ham-and-cheese sandwich that is one of the greatest snacks ever, when traditionally France is not a country of great snackers. Instead, most people in France tend to eat at set mealtimes and observe long-established meal rituals.

The French do, however, excel in the variety of *hors d'oeuvres* they serve for the first course. The phrase '*hors d'oeuvres*' means 'outside the main work', as these dishes whet the appetite before the serious eating begins. Pâtés and terrines, savoury hot or cold tarts, salads, cold meats, shellfish and a seemingly infinite variety of soups are among the traditional French first courses. Starters in restaurants tend to be more elaborate than those served at home unless, of course, company is expected. Mixed Salad Selection (see page 49), Celeriac Rémoulade with Ham (see page 46), Chicory and Pear Salad (see page 69) and the Country-style Terrine (see page 54) are examples of everyday first courses for eating *en famille* or at small bistros.

The versatile recipes in this chapter – many of which can do double duty as starters or snacks – have been selected with busy cooks in mind. Most can be prepared ahead and none are difficult. Many recipes are also ideal for light lunches that need nothing more than a few slices of bread or a dressed salad to make a delicious meal.

Soups (*soupes* or *potages*) are an important part of a French meal. In fact, the word 'supper' comes from *souper*, which means 'to take soup', a legacy from when the large midday meal meant only soup was served in the evening. Even today, an informal way of calling diners to the table is still to use the phrase '*à la soupe*'. Most French restaurant menus list a soup of the day (*soupe du jour*), be it vegetable, meat, poultry or seafood. Les Halles Onion Soup (see page 37), with its golden, bubbling melted cheese topping, from Paris, and Vegetable and Bean Soup (see page 40), from sunny Provence, are popular around the world. The Cream of Watercress Soup (see page 38), with its peppery flavour, is an example of French cooks' knack of transforming a simple vegetable into a sophisticated first course. However, Vichyssoise, the chilled leek and potato soup that is widely regarded as one of the great traditional French soups, was, in fact, created at the Ritz-Carlton Hotel in New York City in 1910, albeit by a French chef.

For a French dinner party starter with style and impact, nothing beats light-as-air soufflés straight from the oven. Despite an undeserved reputation as being difficult to prepare, soufflés are surprisingly easy and Spinach Soufflés (see page 42) will kick off any meal with a French flavour.

France's beautiful, unspoilt landscape is the source of some of the finest cuisine and wines to be found anywhere

34

International fast-food outlets are making slow inroads into the French lifestyle, but they do face great resistance. The peckish French are still more likely to snack on a ham and cheese baguette than a mass-produced hamburger. For other French alternatives to the hamburger, try a *tartine*, which consists of toasted or plain bread with any variety of toppings, like the Pear and Roquefort Open-face Sandwiches (see page 48). The French choose *tartines* at many times of the day. Toasted thin French bread (*ficelle*), spread with butter for breakfast, is a *tartine beurrée*, while schoolchildren are often given a mid-morning snack of toasted bread with jam called a *tartine de confiture*. As the day progresses, toppings become savoury and provide a quick lunch for office workers. Wine bar menus, for example, feature *tartines de fromage*, matching regional wines and cheeses. The list of suitable *tartine* ingredients is limitless and *tartines* are an excellent way of utilizing small amounts of leftover cheeses, sliced meats and sausages. Alternatively, spread a slice of French or sourdough bread with Tapenade (see page 60) for a filling snack that takes next-to-no-time to make. The ultimate hot French sandwich, however, has to be the traditional Croque Monsieur (see page 70) with its creamy white sauce topping and ham filling. For another bread-based snack, try a slice of French bread spread with Chicken Liver Pâté (see page 50) or topped with Onion Marmalade (see page 242).

Friends coming round for drinks? How about Tarts Flambé (see page 63), Alsace's version of pizza with a rich crème fraîche, onion and lardon topping, or Baked Vacherin (see page 68)? Both are hassle-free snacks to share. And for a real French-style start to any meal or gathering, serve Champagne flutes of Kir (see page 61).

Even large commercial ports like Marseille have a well-deserved reputation for their seafood

More like a thick onion stew than a liquid soup, this traditional recipe recalls the days when the Les Halles district of Paris was home to the city's meat, seafood and fruit and veg markets, and known as the 'belly of Paris'. All-night cafés catered for market workers, as well as revellers returning home in the early morning hours – the slug of brandy in each bowl of soup might be the source of the soup's legendary restorative qualities.

SERVES 4

85 g/3 oz butter

2 tbsp olive oil

750 g/1 lb 10 oz onions, thinly sliced

1 tsp sugar

1/2 tsp salt

1 1/2 tbsp plain flour

600 ml/1 pint hot beef stock

4 tbsp brandy

125 g/4 1/2 oz Gruyère cheese, or half Gruyère and half Parmesan cheese, grated

salt and pepper

for the Croûtes*

8 slices French bread, about 1 cm/1/2 inch thick

1 garlic clove, halved

1 Melt the butter with the oil in a large heavy-based saucepan with a tight-fitting lid or a flameproof casserole over a medium-high heat. Stir in the onions, sugar and salt, then reduce the heat to low. Cover the surface with a piece of wet greaseproof paper or the lid and cook for 20–30 minutes, stirring occasionally, until the onions are a rich, dark golden brown. Uncover and stir constantly when they start to darken as they can burn easily.

les halles onion soup
soupe à l'oignon les halles

37

2 Sprinkle the flour over the onions and continue cooking, stirring, for a further 2 minutes. Stir in the hot stock and simmer, partially covered, for a further 15 minutes, skimming the surface if necessary.

3 To make the Croûtes, preheat the grill to high and preheat the oven to 200°C/400°F/Gas Mark 6. Arrange the bread slices on the grill rack and toast for 1–2 minutes until golden and crisp. Flip the slices over and repeat on the other side. Rub the top of each bread slice while it is still hot with the garlic halves, then set aside.

4 Stir the brandy into the soup and season to taste with salt and pepper. At this point the soup can be left for up to a day, reheating it before proceeding.

5 Divide the toasted bread between 4 flameproof soup bowls. Ladle over the soup, then top each with a quarter of the cheese. Place the bowls in the oven for 20 minutes, or until the cheese is golden and bubbling. Leave the soup to stand for a couple of minutes before serving.

*cook's tip
The toasted Croûtes are a good way to use up day-old French bread. Take care, however, not to cut the bread too thick or it will absorb all the liquid.

cream of watercress soup
velouté de cresson

The inclusion of the word velouté in the French title indicates that this soup will have a smooth, velvety texture.

SERVES 4

225 g/8 oz fresh watercress, rinsed and any yellow
  or shaggy leaves discarded

40 g/1¹/₂ oz unsalted butter

¹/₂ tbsp sunflower oil

225 g/8 oz floury potatoes, such as King Edward,
  peeled and diced

1 leek, white part only, halved, rinsed and finely sliced

175 ml/6 fl oz dry white wine

700 ml/1¹/₄ pints vegetable stock

175 ml/6 fl oz double cream

1 large egg yolk

salt and pepper

2 tbsp crème fraîche, lightly beaten until smooth,
  to garnish

1 Chop the watercress leaves and stems, reserving a few leaves for a garnish, then set aside. Melt the butter with the oil in a large heavy-based saucepan with a lid over a medium heat. Add the potatoes and leek and stir them around for 2 minutes, or until they are absorbing the butter, but are not coloured.

2 Add the wine and bring to the boil, boiling until it reduces by half. Pour in the stock and return the mixture to the boil, stirring. Reduce the heat to low and leave the soup to simmer, partially covered, for 25 minutes, or until the potato is tender enough to be falling apart.

3 Add the watercress leaves and stems and simmer for 3 minutes, or until the stems are tender. Remove the soup from the heat and transfer it to a food mill, food processor or blender and process until it is smooth.

4 Strain the soup though a fine sieve into a bowl, using the back of a wooden spoon to press it through the sieve. This is easiest to do in small batches. Return the soup to the rinsed saucepan and heat to just below boiling point.

5 Put the cream and egg yolk in a large heatproof bowl and whisk until blended. Add a ladleful of the hot, but not boiling, soup and whisk it in briskly. Add another 2 ladlefuls of soup, whisking briskly, then whisk this mixture into the remaining soup in the pan.* Season to taste with salt and pepper.

6 Just before serving, reheat the soup without boiling, then ladle it into warmed bowls. Lightly swirl a little crème fraîche into each bowl, then add a few of the reserved watercress leaves as a garnish. Serve at once.

*cook's tip
The liaison of cream and egg in Step 5 gives this soup its richness and texture. Adding the ladlefuls of hot soup to the egg mixture, rather than stirring the cream and egg directly into the soup, reduces the risk of the egg curdling. Once the egg has been added to the simmering soup, it is important not to let the soup boil again or it will curdle.

40

vegetable and bean soup
soupe au pistou

From Nice, this thick and hearty soup is a celebration of the best of Provençal produce markets. It takes its name from the fragrant basil sauce stirred in at the last minute, sauce pistou, which is similar to pesto sauce from neighbouring Italy. Jars of prepared pistou from French supermarkets make good souvenirs to bring back from a holiday, but nothing is comparable to the flavour of the freshly made sauce. This soup is also a busy cook's dream in that it tastes best made in advance and then reheated for serving, although the colours won't be as vibrant as when it is freshly made. Do not add the pasta until the soup is ready to reheat.

SERVES 4-6

225 g/8 oz fresh broad beans

2 tbsp olive oil

2 large garlic cloves, crushed

1 large onion, finely chopped

1 celery stick, finely chopped

1 carrot, peeled and chopped

175 g/6 oz firm new potatoes, such as Charlotte, diced

850 ml/1½ pints Vegetable Stock

2 large, juicy beef tomatoes, peeled, deseeded
   and chopped*

1 large bunch of fresh basil, tied together with
   kitchen string

200 g/7 oz courgettes, diced

200 g/7 oz French beans, topped and tailed and chopped

55 g/2 oz dried vermicelli, broken into pieces, or small
   pasta shapes

salt and pepper

extra-virgin olive oil (optional), to garnish

for the Pistou Sauce

100 g/3½ oz fresh basil leaves

2 large garlic cloves

1½ tbsp pine kernels

50 ml/2 fl oz fruity extra-virgin olive oil

55 g/2 oz Parmesan cheese, finely grated

1 If the broad beans are very young and tender, they can be used as they are. If they are older, however, it is best to remove the grey outer skin before cooking. To do this, use a small, sharp knife to slit the grey skins, then 'pop' out the green beans.

2 Heat the olive oil in a large heavy-based saucepan with a tight-fitting lid or flameproof casserole over a medium heat. Add the garlic, onion, celery and carrot and sauté for 5–8 minutes until the onion is soft, but not brown.

3 Add the potatoes, stock and tomatoes and season to taste with salt and pepper. Bring the stock to the boil, skimming the surface if necessary, then add the basil. Reduce the heat and cover the pan. Leave to simmer for 15 minutes, or until the potatoes are tender.

4 Meanwhile, make the Pistou Sauce. Put the basil, garlic and pine kernels in a food processor or blender and blitz until a thick paste forms. Add the extra-virgin olive oil and blitz again. Transfer to a bowl and stir in the cheese, then cover and chill until required.

5 When the potatoes are tender, stir the broad beans, courgettes, French beans and vermicelli into the soup and continue simmering for 10 minutes, or until the vegetables are tender and the pasta is cooked. Taste, and adjust the seasoning if necessary. Remove and discard the bunch of basil.

6 Ladle the soup into bowls and add a spoonful of Pistou Sauce to each bowl. Drizzle with a little extra-virgin olive oil, if you like.

*cook's tip

To peel and deseed the tomatoes, cut a cross in each
tomato at the stem end, then put them in a heatproof
bowl. Pour over enough boiling water to cover and leave
to stand for 30 seconds, or until the skins begin
splitting. Pour off the water and cover the tomatoes
with cold water to stop them from cooking. The skins
will now peel off easily. Cut each tomato in half, then
use a teaspoon to scoop out the cores and seeds.

42

spinach soufflés
soufflés aux épinards

*Serving billowing hot soufflés for a first course gives
any meal an unmistakable French start. Soufflés have
an undeserved reputation for being difficult, but it
is true that they must be served quickly before they
deflate and all the impact is lost. Have your guests
seated at the table and wine poured a minute or two
before the soufflés are due to come out of the oven.*

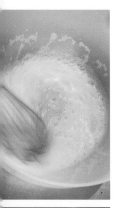

MAKES 4

1 tbsp fine dry breadcrumbs

30 g/1 oz unsalted butter

1 spring onion, finely chopped

140 g/5 oz fresh spinach leaves, thick stems removed
   and well rinsed

15 g/½ oz plain flour

125 ml/4 fl oz hot milk

freshly grated nutmeg

2 large eggs, separated

40 g/1½ oz Gruyère cheese, finely grated

¼ tsp cream of tartar

salt and pepper

1 Preheat the oven to 200°C/400°F/Gas Mark 6 with
a baking tray inside. Lightly grease the sides of
4 x 150-ml/5-fl oz ramekins, then very lightly sprinkle
breadcrumbs around the side of each, tapping out
the excess.

2 Melt 15 g/½ oz of the butter in a heavy-based
saucepan over a medium heat. Add the spring
onion and stir for 1–2 minutes until it is soft, but
not brown.

3 Add the spinach to the saucepan with just the
rinsing water clinging to its leaves. Add a pinch of
salt and cook, stirring, until the leaves wilt and the
excess water evaporates. Remove the saucepan from the
heat and set aside for the spinach to cool.

4 Melt the remaining butter in a saucepan over a
medium heat. Add the flour and cook, whisking, for
2 minutes. Remove the saucepan from the heat and
slowly whisk in the milk. Season the sauce generously
with salt, pepper and nutmeg.

5 Return the saucepan to the heat, increase the heat
to medium-high and continue whisking for 1 minute,
or until the sauce thickens. Remove the saucepan from
the heat and whisk in the egg yolks, one-by-one.

6 Squeeze the spinach to remove any excess
liquid, then chop it very finely. Stir the spinach
and 30 g/1 oz of the cheese into the sauce.

7 Put the egg whites in a spotlessly clean bowl and
beat until they are broken up and frothy. Beat in the
cream of tartar, then gradually increase the speed of the
beating until stiff peaks form.* Use a large metal spoon
or rubber spatula to beat 1 spoonful of the whites into
the spinach mixture. Spoon the remaining whites on top
of the spinach and lightly fold them in, using a figure-
of-eight motion.

8 Divide the mixture equally between the ramekins,
filling each about three-quarters full. Tap the dishes
lightly on the work surface, then sprinkle the tops with
the remaining cheese. Place the soufflés on the hot
baking tray and put in the oven.

9 Immediately reduce the oven temperature to
190°C/375°F/Gas Mark 5 and bake for 15 minutes,
or until the soufflés are risen and golden on top. Place
each soufflé on a plate and serve at once.

*cook's tip
It's easy to tell when the egg whites are beaten stiffly
enough in Step 7. Hold the bowl upside down and, if the
whites don't start to slide out, they are ready to use.

mixed herb omelette
omelette aux fines herbes

Omelettes are fast food – with French flair. A mixture of finely chopped herbs called fines herbes is one traditional flavouring, but this version from a stylish Paris restaurant uses the same herbs whole. A perfect omelette is golden brown on the bottom and slightly soft in the centre.

SERVES 1

2 large eggs

2 tbsp milk

40 g/1½ oz butter

1 sprig of fresh flat-leaf parsley, stem bruised

leaves from 1 sprig of fresh flat-leaf parsley

1 sprig of fresh chervil

2 fresh chives

salt and pepper

1 Break the eggs into a bowl. Add the milk and salt and pepper to taste, and quickly beat until just blended.

2 Heat a 20-cm/8-inch omelette pan or frying pan over a medium-high heat until it is very hot and you can feel the heat rising from the surface. Add 30 g/1 oz of the butter and use a fork to rub it over the base and around the sides as it melts.

3 As soon as the butter stops sizzling, pour in the eggs. Shake the pan forwards and backwards over the heat and use the fork to stir the eggs around the pan in a circular motion. Do not scrape the base of the pan.

4 As the omelette begins to set, use the fork to push the cooked egg from the edge towards the centre, so the remaining uncooked egg comes in contact with the hot base of the pan. Continue doing this for 3 minutes, or until the omelette looks set on the bottom, but is still slightly runny on top.

From mountain peak to forest floor: the varied scenery on offer in France is mirrored by the range of the cuisine

5 Place the herbs in the centre of the omelette. Tilt the pan away from the handle, so the omelette slides towards the edge of the pan. Use the fork to fold the top half of the omelette over the herbs. Slide the omelette onto a plate, then rub the remaining butter over the top. Omelettes are best eaten immediately.

variations

For a more traditional *omelette aux fines herbes*, finely chop the parsley, chervil and some tarragon leaves and snip the chives, then fold them into the egg mixture in Step 1.

Other suitable fillings for omelettes include hot Ratatouille, Sautéed Mushrooms or a grated cheese such as Gruyère or sliced goat's cheese.

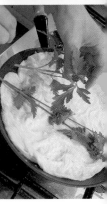

celeriac rémoulade with ham
céleri rémoulade au jambon

Although sold ready-made in charcuteries *and supermarkets, this universally popular French salad of celeriac with mustard-flavoured mayonnaise is also often made at home. It is traditionally served as a first course, often as part of an* assiette de crudités, *but it also makes a good sandwich filling on a sliced baguette with ham slices.*

SERVES 4–6

1¹/₂ tsp lemon juice

1 tsp salt

1 large celeriac, about 450 g/1 lb

1¹/₂ tbsp capers in brine, rinsed, dried and
    chopped (optional)

8 thin slices salt-cured ham, such as Bayonne, to serve

chopped fresh parsley, to garnish

for the Rémoulade Sauce

1 large egg yolk

1–1¹/₂ tbsp Dijon mustard, to taste

¹/₂ tsp red wine vinegar

150 ml/5 fl oz sunflower oil

salt and pepper

1 To make the Rémoulade Sauce, put the egg yolk, 1 tablespoon of the mustard and the red wine vinegar in a food processor or blender and whiz until blended. With the motor still running, pour the oil through the feed tube, drop by drop, until the mayonnaise starts to thicken. At that point you can add the oil in a slow, steady stream. Add salt and pepper to taste, along with more mustard, if necessary. Transfer to a large bowl, then cover and chill until required.

2 To prepare the celeriac, put the lemon juice and salt in a large bowl of water. Peel the celeriac and cut it into quarters, then use the slicing disc of a food processor or a hand grater to thinly shred. Add the celeriac to the acidulated water as it is shredded, to prevent discolouration.

3 Drain the celeriac well and pat dry before stirring it into the Rémoulade Sauce. Stir in the capers, if using, and leave the salad to stand for 20 minutes at room temperature, then adjust the seasoning if necessary.

4 To serve, arrange 2 slices of ham on each plate and spoon a mound of celeriac next to it, then sprinkle with parsley.

variations

If you don't have enough ham to serve it on the side, thinly slice what you have, stir it into the Celeriac Rémoulade and serve with slices of French bread. Plain cooked ham, Italian Parma ham or Spanish Serrano ham are also good to use.

You can serve the celeriac mixture on shredded radicchio or chicory leaves.

For a more robust flavour, add 3–5 drained canned anchovy fillets to the egg yolk, mustard and red wine vinegar in Step 1.

Stir in 1 can (200 g/7 oz) well-drained crabmeat instead of ham.

48 pear and roquefort open-face sandwiches
tartines aux poires et roquefort

When it comes to devising quick snacks, the French have the answer with tartines. *These are open-face sandwiches that are toasted or not, and the list of suitable ingredients is limitless. Any bread is fine to use for this, but for fussy Parisians,* pain Poilâne, *a dense sourdough bread with a chewy crust, is a must.*

MAKES 2

4 slices walnut bread or pain Poilâne, about
  1 cm/½ inch thick
4 thin slices cured ham, such as Bayonne or Parma
2 ripe pears, such as Conference, peeled, halved, cored
  and thinly sliced lengthways
100 g/3½ oz Roquefort cheese, very thinly sliced
mixed salad leaves
Walnut Vinaigrette

1 Preheat the grill to high. Put the bread slices under the grill and toast until crisp, but not brown, on both sides. Do not turn off the grill.

2 Fold or cut the ham slices to cover each slice of bread, then equally divide the pear slices between the *tartines*. Lay the cheese slices on top.

3 Return the *tartines* to the grill until the cheese melts and bubbles. Mix the salad leaves with the Walnut Vinaigrette and serve 1 or 2 *tartines* per portion with the salad on the side.

variations

As most French people buy bread daily, they always have on hand the essential ingredient to create an almost instant meal from a few ingredients and lots of imagination. For a crunchy snack in a flash, try a slice of sourdough bread spread with salted butter and topped with thinly sliced new-season radishes and a sprinkling of finely chopped parsley.

other ideas include:

Cut a baguette in half lengthways, then cut into 13-cm/5-inch pieces and toast. Spread each slice with Tapenade and then top with Ratatouille.

Spread Onion Marmalade over slices of *pain Poilâne* or crusty white bread, then top with slices of goat's cheese. The *tartines* are ready to eat or they can be put under a preheated hot grill until the cheese melts.

For an quick alternative to a traditional Croque Monsieur, top toasted slices of bread with cooked ham and thin slices of Comté cheese and grill until the cheese melts and bubbles.

Spread thick slices of untoasted bread with salted butter and top with a selection of thinly sliced cooked or smoked sausages.

mixed salad selection
assiette de crudités

Most French cafés and bistros include a selection of salads such as these on the menu. This is an excellent choice to serve before any rich main course or as a light lunch.

SERVES 4–6

Celeriac Rémoulade

for the Carrot Salad

450 g/1 lb carrots, peeled

2 tbsp olive oil

2 tbsp freshly squeezed orange juice

2 tbsp finely chopped almonds

1 tbsp finely chopped fresh flat-leaf parsley

salt and pepper

for the Beetroot Salad

400 g/14 oz cooked beetroot, peeled

2 tbsp Vinaigrette

1 tbsp snipped fresh chives

to serve

slices French bread

unsalted butter

1 To make the Carrot Salad, use the slicing disc of a food processor or a hand grater to finely shred the carrots. Put the carrots in a bowl with the olive oil and orange juice and toss together. Season the salad to taste with salt and pepper and cover and chill until required. Stir in the almonds and parsley just before serving.

2 To make the Beetroot Salad, cut the beetroot into 5-mm/¼-inch slices. Stack several of the beetroot slices and cut vertically into 5-mm/¼-inch batons, then cut the batons into dice, continuing until all the beetroots are diced. Put the beetroot in a bowl, add the Vinaigrette and toss together. Cover and chill until required. Stir in the chives just before serving.

3 To serve, divide the Celeriac Rémoulade, Carrot Salad and Beetroot Salad between individual plates and accompany with plenty of French bread and butter.

variations

A slice of Ham and Parsley Terrine goes well with this selection of salads.

To give the Carrot Salad a Moroccan flavour, add ½ teaspoon of ground cumin with the oil and orange juice.

When young fresh radishes are in season, include a scrubbed bunch with the greens still attached and a pot of sea salt for dipping them in.

50

chicken liver pâté
pâté de foie de volailles

The richness of this smooth, elegant version of chicken liver pâté belies its simplicity. For anyone new to pâté-making, this is the place to start. In French bistros, this pâté is served with a crock of cornichons, a basket of French bread and pots of unsalted butter for spreading on the bread with the pâté. Croûtes and Onion Marmalade also go well with it, as do the salad and toasted brioche suggested here.

MAKES 8–10 SLICES

175 g/6 oz unsalted butter

500 g/1 lb 2 oz chicken livers, thawed if frozen,
  and trimmed

¹/₂ tbsp sunflower oil

2 shallots, finely chopped

2 large garlic cloves, finely chopped

2¹/₂ tbsp Madeira or brandy

2 tbsp double cream

1 tsp dried thyme

¹/₄ tsp ground allspice

salt and pepper

chopped fresh flat-leaf parsley, to garnish

to serve

toasted slices brioche

mixed salad leaves

Raspberry Vinaigrette

1 Melt 30 g/1 oz of the butter in a large sauté or frying pan over a medium-high heat. Add the chicken livers and stir for 5 minutes, or until they are brown on the outside, but still slightly pink in the centres. Work in batches, if necessary, to avoid overcrowding the pan.

2 Transfer the livers and their cooking juices to a food processor. Melt another 30 g/1 oz of the butter with the oil in the pan. Add the shallots and garlic and sauté, stirring frequently, for 2–3 minutes until the shallots are soft, but not brown.

3 Add the Madeira to the pan and scrape up any cooking juices from the base. Stir in the cream, then stir in the thyme, allspice and salt and pepper to taste. Pour this mixture into the food processor with the livers, scraping in all of the cooking juices. Add the remaining butter, cut into small pieces.

4 Whiz the mixture in the food processor until smooth. Taste, and adjust the seasoning if necessary. Leave the mixture to cool slightly, then scrape into a serving bowl and set aside for the pâté to cool completely.

5 When the pâté is cool, it can be served straightaway or the surface covered with clingfilm and chilled for up to 3 days. Leave at room temperature for 30 minutes before serving.

6 Just before serving, sprinkle the surface with parsley, then serve with hot toasted brioche and the salad leaves tossed with the Raspberry Vinaigrette.*

*cook's tip
If you aren't going to serve the pâté within 3 days, arrange some herbs, such as thyme sprigs or bay leaves, decoratively on top and pour over a layer of Clarified Butter. The butter acts as a seal and will keep the pâté fresh for up to 5 days in the refrigerator. Serve in scoops, straight from the bowl.

ham and parsley terrine 53
jambon persillé

*Pretty with bright green flecks and chunks of pale
pink ham, this traditional Easter dish from Burgundy
is, in fact, sold year-round at charcuteries all over
France. It is certainly convenient to buy slices by
weight, but not difficult to make at home.*

MAKES 15–20 SLICES

4 gelatine leaves

350 ml/12 fl oz dry white wine, such as Chablis

250 ml/9 fl oz warm water

30 g/1 oz unsalted butter

2 shallots, very finely chopped

1 garlic clove, crushed

40 g/1¹/₂ oz fresh flat-leaf parsley, finely chopped

300 g/10¹/₂ oz piece of ham, cut into
  1-cm/¹/₂-inch dice

pepper

1 Put the gelatine leaves in a bowl with enough
cold water to cover and leave to soak for 5 minutes.
Meanwhile, put the wine and water in a saucepan and
heat just until small bubbles begin to appear around the
edge, without boiling.

2 Melt the butter in a saucepan over a medium
heat. Add the shallots and garlic and fry, stirring
frequently, for 3 minutes, or until soft, but not brown.
Transfer to a heatproof bowl and set aside. Stir the
parsley into the bowl and add pepper to taste.

3 Use your hands to lift the gelatine leaves out of the
cold water and squeeze to remove the excess liquid.
Remove the pan with the simmering liquid from the
heat, add the gelatine and stir until it dissolves. Add the
liquid to the parsley mixture.

4 Rinse the inside of a 1.5-litre/2³/₄-pint rectangular
terrine with water and do not dry.* Pour a
5-mm/¹/₄-inch layer of the herbed gelatine mixture
in the base of the terrine and put in the refrigerator
for 30 minutes, or until beginning to set.

5 Scatter one-third of the ham pieces over the set
layer of gelatine, pressing the ham slightly into
the gelatine. Return the terrine to the refrigerator for
30 minutes, or until the gelatine is set.

6 Top the layer of ham with one-third of the
remaining gelatine mixture, then return to the
refrigerator until starting to set. Add another third of
the ham and return to the refrigerator for 30 minutes,
or until set. Continue layering and chilling until all the
ingredients are used, ending with a layer of herbed
gelatine. Cover the terrine and leave to chill at least
overnight, or for up to 2 days.

7 To serve, run a round-bladed knife around the edge.
Place a serving dish on top of the terrine, then
carefully invert both, giving a sharp shake halfway over,
and lift off the terrine. Cut into slices and serve.

*cook's tip
Rinsing the terrine with water helps it turn out easily
and smoothly. If, however, there isn't a clear thump
when the terrine is inverted in Step 7, set the terrine
in a sink of hot water for 20–30 seconds, then invert
and turn out.

54 country-style terrine
terrine de campagne

The French are Europe's undisputed masters of pâté and terrine making, and coarse terrines, such as this version, feature on small restaurant menus throughout the country. These well-flavoured, mixed-meat combinations are surprisingly easy to prepare and keep for several days, which makes them just as ideal for home cooks as for restaurateurs.

MAKES 15–20 SLICES

350 g/12 oz coarsely minced fresh pork

250 g/9 oz coarsely minced fresh veal

200 g/7 oz pig's liver, finely chopped

200 g/7 oz pork fat, diced

125 ml/4 fl oz brandy

2 large garlic cloves, very finely chopped

2 tbsp chopped fresh flat-leaf parsley

1 tsp salt

³/₄ tsp dried thyme

large pinch of ground allspice

10–12 unsmoked streaky bacon rashers, rinds removed

55 g/2 oz shelled pistachio nuts, roughly chopped

2 skinless, boneless chicken breasts, about

  175 g/6 oz each, cut into thin strips

small handful of fresh chives

pepper

1 Put the pork, veal, pig's liver, pork fat, brandy, garlic, parsley, salt, thyme, allspice and pepper to taste in a large bowl and use your hands to mix together. Cover the bowl with clingfilm and chill for at least 8 or for up to 24 hours.

2 Preheat the oven to 160°C/325°F/Gas Mark 3. Lightly grease the base and sides of a 1.5-litre/2³/₄-pint rectangular cast-iron terrine.* Put the bacon rashers on a chopping board and use the back of a knife to stretch them until they almost double in length. Use the rashers to line the base and sides of the terrine, laying the rashers next to each other, so that the excess hangs over both long sides of the terrine.

3 To check if the seasoning of the meat mixture needs adjusting, heat a small frying pan over a medium-high heat and fry a small amount of the mixture. Taste, and adjust the seasoning if necessary, then stir the pistachio nuts into the meat mixture.

4 Spoon one-third of the meat mixture into the terrine, pressing it down well. Lay half the chicken breast slices on top, pointing from short end to short end, and add a few chives, pointing in the same direction. Repeat this layering, ending with a layer of the meat mixture.

5 Fold over the overhanging strips of bacon so that they cover the top of the meat mixture. Cover the terrine with the cast-iron lid and put in a roasting tin. Bring a kettle of water to the boil and pour enough water into the roasting tin to come halfway up the sides of the terrine .

6 Transfer the roasting tin to the oven and cook for 1¹/₂ hours, or until the mixture pulls away from the side of the terrine and the juices run clear. When a metal skewer is put through the small hole in the terrine lid, it should come out hot.

7 Remove the terrine from the water and leave it to stand for 5 minutes. Uncover the terrine and pour off most of the excess juices, then set it aside to cool completely.

8 While the terrine is cooling, cut a piece of cardboard to fit the top. Put the cardboard in position and place 3 cans of vegetables or beans on top. Alternatively, position a loaf tin on top and put 3 cans in it. Place the terrine and weights in the refrigerator and leave for at least 24 hours, and preferably 48 hours, to set and for the flavours to blend.

Overleaf Watching the world go by while dining outside is one of France's great pleasures

9 To serve, run a round-bladed knife around the edge of the terrine to loosen, then set the base of the terrine in a sink of very hot water for 20–30 seconds. Place a serving dish on top of the terrine, then carefully invert both, giving a sharp shake halfway over, and lift off the terrine. Leave the terrine to return to room temperature, then use a serrated knife to slice.

cook's tip

If you don't have a cast-iron terrine, use a 23 x 13-cm/ 9 x 5-inch loaf tin covered tightly with a double thickness of greased foil. Check for doneness after 1³/₄ hours, although the terrine might take up to 2¹/₄ hours to cook through.

leek and goat's cheese crêpes
crêpes aux poireaux et chèvre

MAKES 8

30 g/1 oz unsalted butter

½ tbsp sunflower oil

200 g/7 oz leeks, halved, rinsed and finely shredded

freshly grated nutmeg, to taste

1 tbsp finely snipped fresh chives

8 Savoury Crêpes

85 g/3 oz soft goat's cheese, rind removed
  if necessary, chopped

salt and pepper

Just as French crêperies are the ideal places to go for quick, inexpensive meals, making crêpes at home provides endless variety at mealtimes and the choice of fillings is only limited by your imagination. Vegetarians often have a difficult time eating out in France, but this is one dish that fits the bill.
To make fresh Crêpes turn to page 247.

1 Preheat the oven to 200°C/400°F/Gas Mark 6. Melt the butter with the oil in a heavy-based saucepan with a lid over a medium-high heat. Add the leeks and stir around so that they are well coated. Stir in salt and pepper to taste, but remember the cheese might be salty. Add a few gratings of nutmeg, then cover the leeks with a sheet of wet greaseproof paper and put the lid on the saucepan. Reduce the heat to very low and leave the leeks to sweat for 5–7 minutes until very tender, but not brown. Stir in the chives, then taste and adjust the seasoning if necessary.

2 Put 1 crêpe on the work surface and put one-eighth of the leeks on the crêpe, top with one-eighth of the cheese, then fold the crêpe into a square parcel or simply roll it around the filling. Place the stuffed crêpe on a baking tray, then continue to fill and fold or roll the remaining crêpes.

3 Put the baking tray in the oven and bake for 5 minutes, or until the crêpes are hot and the cheese starts to melt. Serve hot.

variation
Roll the crêpes around reheated Ratatouille. Grate fresh Parmesan cheese over the top before putting in the oven in Step 3.

cherry tomato clafoutis

clafoutis de tomates cerise

Clafoutis is a baked batter pudding more traditionally made with cherries. Normally it is found among the desserts on French menus, but young chefs are giving the clafoutis new twists and serving it as a savoury first course. Here, bright-red cherry tomatoes are baked in cheese-flavoured clafoutis batter. This can be served hot or warm.

SERVES 4–6

400 g/14 oz cherry tomatoes

3 tbsp chopped fresh flat-leaf parsley, snipped
  fresh chives or finely shredded fresh basil

100 g/3^1/$_2$ oz Gruyère cheese, grated

55 g/2 oz plain flour

4 large eggs, lightly beaten

3 tbsp crème fraîche

225 ml/8 fl oz milk

salt and pepper

1 Preheat the oven to 190°C/375°F/Gas Mark 5.
Lightly grease an oval 1.5-litre/2^3/$_4$-pint ovenproof dish.* Arrange the cherry tomatoes in the dish and sprinkle with the herbs and half the cheese.

2 Put the flour in a mixing bowl, then slowly add the eggs, whisking until smooth. Whisk in the crème fraîche, then slowly whisk in the milk to make a thin, smooth batter. Season to taste with salt and pepper.

3 Gently pour the batter over the tomatoes, then sprinkle the top with the remaining cheese. Bake for 40–45 minutes until set and puffy, covering the top with foil if it browns too much before the batter sets. Leave the clafoutis to cool for a few minutes before cutting to serve hot, or leave to cool to room temperature.

*cook's tip

Put the ovenproof dish with the cherry tomatoes on a baking tray before you add the batter. That way it is easier to transfer to the oven without spilling the batter.

60

tapenade
tapenade

An unmistakable taste of sunny southern France. This ever-so-versatile, jet-black spread takes its name from the Provençal word for a caper, tapéno, *yet the main ingredient is always olives, while capers and anchovies are usually included, but are optional. Most Provençal restaurateurs provide a small pot of this pungent, gutsy tapenade to enjoy with drinks before a meal, but it is also used to flavour roast lamb, meat stews and tarts, or served as a dip with a selection of crisp, fresh vegetables.*

MAKES ABOUT 300 G/10¹/₂ OZ

250 g/9 oz black olives, such as Nyons or Niçoise, stoned

3 anchovy fillets in oil, drained

1 large garlic clove, halved, with the green centre removed, if necessary

2 tbsp pine kernels

¹/₂ tbsp capers in brine, rinsed

125 ml/4 fl oz extra-virgin olive oil

freshly squeezed lemon or orange juice, to taste

pepper

for the Garlic Croûtes

12 slices French bread, about 5 mm/¹/₄ inch thick

extra-virgin olive oil

2 garlic cloves, peeled but left whole

1 Put the olives, anchovy fillets, garlic, pine kernels and capers in a food processor or blender and whiz until well blended. With the motor still running, pour the olive oil through the feed tube and continue blending until a loose paste forms.

2 Add the lemon juice and pepper to taste. It shouldn't need any salt because of the saltiness of the anchovies. Cover and chill until required.*

3 To make the Garlic Croûtes, preheat the grill to high. Place the bread slices on the grill rack and toast one side for 1–2 minutes until golden brown. Flip the bread slices over, lightly brush the untoasted side with olive oil, then toast for 1–2 minutes.

4 Rub 1 side of each bread slice with the garlic cloves while it is still hot, then set aside and leave to cool completely. Store in an airtight container for up to 2 days.

5 Serve the tapenade with the Garlic Croûtes.

*cook's tip
Any leftover tapenade can be stored in a covered container in the refrigerator for up to a week. Pour a thin layer of olive oil over the surface before covering.

kir
kir

One of the most popular apéritifs in France, Kir is a refreshing chilled drink made with a dry white wine from Burgundy and crème de cassis, *a garnet-red blackcurrant liqueur, produced primarily around Dijon. When the* crème de cassis *is mixed with Champagne or a sparkling wine, the drink becomes a kir royale. If cassis is the best known of the numerous fruit liqueurs made in France, it has Canon Felix Kir, a priest and post-war mayor of Dijon, to thank for its popularity. To revive flagging cassis sales, Canon Kir created this eponymous drink, mixing white wine made from the Aligoté grape with the liqueur. He then served it to visiting international dignitaries and the rest, as they say, is history.*

SERVES 1

1 part crème de cassis

4 parts chilled dry white wine, such as Aligoté
  or Chardonnay

1 Pour the cassis into a wine glass, then top up with the chilled white wine and stir to blend.

variations

For a variation on a theme, mix the *crème de cassis* with a red Burgundy wine; the drink then becomes known as a *cardinale*.

The French have a long history of transforming seasonal fruit into sweet liqueurs, many of which are just as suitable to combine with wine as *crème de cassis*. For variations on the kir, try *crème de fraises de bois* (from cultivated 'wild' strawberries), *crème de framboises* (raspberry liqueur), *crème de myrtilles* (bilberry liqueur from southern France) and *crème de pêches* (peach liqueur).

A quiet, tree-lined road and a lone cyclist – could this idyllic scene be anywhere other than rural France?

tarts flambé   63
tartes flambées

Alsatian culinary folklore claims that this thin, pizza-like tart has been a speciality of the region since the sixteenth century. Traditionally, bakers would roll out leftover scraps of dough after shaping loaves of bread, then top the thin dough discs with cream, onions and bacon. The tarts were then put in the wood-fired ovens and by the time they finished baking, the coals were at the correct temperature for bread baking. Serve with a bottle of crisp Alsace Riesling.

SERVES 6–8

125 g/4½ oz smoked lardons

125 ml/4 fl oz crème fraîche

2 onions, very thinly sliced

for the tart base

400 g/14 oz plain flour

1 sachet of easy-blend dried yeast

1 tsp salt

1 tsp sugar

225 ml/8 fl oz water

1 tbsp extra-virgin olive oil

1 To make the tart base, stir the flour, yeast, salt and sugar together in a large mixing bowl and make a well in the centre. Heat the water until it registers 52°C/125°F on an instant-read thermometer, or until it feels warm on the back of your hand. Add the olive oil to the water, then pour it into the well and stir in the flour from the sides to make a soft dough.

2 Turn out the dough onto a lightly floured work surface and knead for 10 minutes, or until smooth and elastic. Shape the dough into a ball and set aside while you wash the bowl and lightly smear the sides with olive oil. Put the dough in the bowl, cover with clingfilm and set aside until it doubles in size, which can take up to an hour.

3 Meanwhile, put the lardons in a large dry sauté or frying pan over a medium-high heat and stir for 3 minutes, or until they just cook and give off their fat, but aren't brown.

4 Preheat the oven to 240°C/475°F/Gas Mark 9 with a baking tray inside. Punch down the dough, turn it out on a lightly floured work surface and quickly knead a few times. Gather back into a ball, cover with the upturned bowl and leave to rest again for 10 minutes.

5 Divide the dough into half. Place 1 half on a lightly floured work surface and roll out into a 30-cm/12-inch round. Transfer the dough round to the hot baking tray and spread half the crème fraîche over the surface, taking it almost to the edge. Sprinkle with half the onions and lardons.

6 Transfer the baking tray to the oven and bake the tart for 12–15 minutes until the crust is golden and the onions char on the tips if the oven is hot enough. Cut into slices and serve at once, then prepare the second tart in the same way.

anchovy and onion tart
pissaladière

There are many variations of this Provençal tart, which was originally made with bread dough rather than a tart case. The French name refers back to when the filling was nothing more than a purée of anchovies and sardines, called a pissala. In Provence, this tart is sold as a snack for munching at any time of the day, to enjoy with apéritifs or as a first course.

SERVES 6–8

1 quantity Savoury Tart Pastry

6 tbsp garlic–flavoured olive oil

1 kg/2 lb 4 oz onions, thinly sliced

¹/₂ tbsp dried thyme leaves

5 tbsp Tapenade, home-made or bought

salt and pepper

to garnish

55 g/2 oz anchovy fillets in oil, drained
  and sliced lengthways

12–15 stoned black olives

1 Remove the pastry from the refrigerator about 10 minutes before you roll it out. Preheat the oven to 200°C/400°F/Gas Mark 6 with a baking tray inside.

2 Roll out the pastry on a lightly floured work surface and use to line a 28 x 20-cm/11 x 8-inch rectangular tart tin. Gently roll a rolling pin over the top of the tin to take off the excess pastry. Line with greaseproof paper and fill with baking beans. Put the tart case on the hot baking tray and bake for 10–15 minutes, or until the rim is set. Remove the paper and beans, then return the tart case to the oven and bake for a further 5 minutes, or until the base looks dry.

3 Meanwhile, heat the oil in a large heavy-based sauté or frying pan with a tight-fitting lid over a medium-high heat. Add the onions and stir around until they are well coated in oil.

4 Reduce the heat to the lowest setting and press a wet piece of greaseproof paper over the surface. Cover tightly with the lid and leave the onions to simmer for 45 minutes, or until very tender. Stir in the thyme leaves and add salt and pepper to taste. Remember the anchovies used to garnish will be salty.

5 While the onions are cooking, reheat the oven to 180°C/350°F/Gas Mark 4. Spread the Tapenade over the base of the pastry.

6 Spoon the onions into the pastry case and spread them out evenly. Arrange the anchovy fillets in a lattice pattern on top and dot with the olives.

7 Return the tart to the oven and bake for 25–30 minutes until the crust is golden. If the pastry begins to brown too much, cover the tart with a sheet of foil. Transfer the tart to a wire rack and leave it to stand for 10 minutes before removing from the tin. Leave to cool completely, then cut into slices.

Busy, bustling marinas are a big feature of the resorts along France's sophisticated southern coast

These individual tarts, with their rich pastry and the simple egg, cheese and lardon filling, are equally good served hot or at room temperature. Simple to make and versatile, they are ideal for first courses, light lunches when served with a salad on the side, for parties or for taking on family picnics.

MAKES 6 12-CM/4¹/₂-INCH TARTS

1 quantity Savoury Tart Pastry
125 g/4¹/₂ oz unsmoked lardons
2 large eggs
225 ml/8 fl oz whipping cream
125 g/4¹/₂ oz Gruyère cheese, grated
freshly grated nutmeg
salt and pepper

1 Remove the pastry from the refrigerator about 10 minutes before you roll it out and preheat the oven to 200°C/400°F/Gas Mark 6 with a baking tray inside.

2 Divide the pastry into 6 equal pieces and roll out each on a lightly floured work surface into 15–18-cm/6–7-inch rounds. Use to line 6 x 12-cm/4¹/₂-inch tart tins, leaving the excess pastry hanging over the edges.* Line the tart cases with greaseproof paper and fill with baking beans. Put the tart cases on the hot baking tray and bake for 5 minutes, or until the rim is set. Remove the paper and beans, then return the tart cases to the oven and bake for a further 5 minutes, or until the bases look dry. Leave the tart cases on the baking tray and remove from the oven. Reduce the oven temperature to 190°C/375°F/Gas Mark 5.

3 Meanwhile, put the lardons in a sauté or frying pan over a low heat and sauté for 3 minutes, or until the fat begins to melt. Increase the heat to medium and continue sautéeing until they are crisp.

quiche lorraine tartlets

67

tartelettes quiche lorraine

4 Sprinkle the lardons over the pastry case. Beat the eggs, cream and cheese together, then season to taste with the salt and pepper and nutmeg. Carefully divide the filling between the pastry cases, then transfer the tarts to the oven to bake for 20–25 minutes until the filling is set and the pastry is golden brown. Transfer the quiches to a wire rack to cool completely, then remove from the tins.

*cook's tip

It is important to handle the pastry as little as possible to prevent it 'shrinking' while it bakes blind. To avoid this, leave the excess pastry hanging over the sides of the tins. Trim away just enough so that it doesn't touch the baking sheet. After the tartlets have baked, gently roll a rolling pin over the top edges and the excess will fall away, leaving a neat edge.

A bird's-eye view of Paris: the French capital is a veritable gastronomic melting pot for the nation's cuisine

68 baked vacherin
vacherin fondu

Vacherin is a creamy, full-fat cheese from the Savoie and Franche-Comté regions of France, usually served as a dessert course. It is so creamy that it often has to be spooned, rather than sliced, onto slices of French bread. Here it is baked to make an ultra-simple, quick version of a cheese fondue to serve with apéritifs or as a first course. Vacherin is sold in thin wooden boxes, from which it is served either when it is baked, as in this recipe, or uncooked as a cheese course.

SERVES 4–6

1 whole Vacherin cheese, in its wooden box,
  at room temperature
1 garlic clove, cut into thin slivers
2 tbsp dry white wine

to serve
24 slices French bread, cubed, or Croûtes
  or Garlic Croûtes
selection of vegetable dippers, such as carrot sticks,
  trimmed radishes and chicory leaves

1 Remove the cheese from the refrigerator and remove the lid and any plastic covering 30 minutes in advance, so that it comes to room temperature. Preheat the oven to 220°C/425°F/Gas Mark 7.

2 Place the box of Vacherin on a piece of foil, shiny-side up, that is large enough to wrap up around the side of the box. Place the wrapped cheese box on a baking tray and make as many slits on the surface as you have garlic slices, then push the garlic slices into the slits.

3 Use a fork to prick the cheese all over, then spoon over the wine. Some of the wine will soak in and some will float on the surface.

4 Bake the wrapped cheese box in the oven for 25 minutes, then transfer the cheese to a serving plate and use a knife to cut open the top. Serve fondue-style with cubes of bread speared on forks and vegetables for dipping into the melted cheese.

chicory and pear salad
salade d'endives et poires

1 To make the Caramelized Walnuts, lightly grease a sheet of foil and put it over a heatproof surface, such as a chopping board.

2 Put the sugar and water in a small heavy-based saucepan over a high heat and stir until the sugar dissolves. Bring to the boil, without stirring, and continue boiling for 10 minutes, or until the caramel turns a dark golden brown. Watch carefully because the caramel can burn quickly.

3 Add the walnuts and use a spoon to stir them until they are coated. Immediately tip them out onto the foil and use the fork to spread them out into a single layer. Work quickly or the caramel will harden and set. Set aside and leave until completely cool.

4 Peel, core and slice the pears lengthways. Brush each slice with a little lemon juice as it is prepared to prevent discolouration.

5 Put the chicory leaves in a bowl and add 4 tablespoons of the Vinaigrette. Use your hands to toss together so that the leaves are all coated. Add extra dressing, if necessary. Add the pear slices and gently toss again.

6 Divide the salad between individual plates, then crumble the cheese over. Chop the walnuts and sprinkle them over to serve.

This bistro favourite – with crisp chicory leaves, juicy pears, creamy Roquefort cheese and walnuts – is a particularly good first course during the autumn and winter when salad leaves aren't at their best. Caramelizing the walnuts is a modern twist.

SERVES 4

2 large pears

juice of ¹/₂ lemon

2 heads of chicory, separated into leaves

4–6 tbsp Vinaigrette (see page 244)

100 g/3¹/₂ oz Roquefort cheese

for the Caramelized Walnuts*

85 g/3 oz caster sugar

2 tbsp water

55 g/2 oz walnut halves

*cook's tip
The Caramelized Walnuts will keep in a covered container for several days at room temperature.

70 croque monsieur
croque monsieur

Is there anything more evocative of eating at a French café than this classic toasted ham and cheese sandwich? It is said the first Croque Monsieur was served in 1910 in a café on the Boulevard des Capucines in Paris, and it's never been off menus since. Unfortunately, today ordinary toasted ham-and-cheese sandwiches are often served as croque monsieurs, but this is the more traditional – indulgent – version. Sandwiches made with long, thin baguettes are an iconic image of French snack food, but for this sandwich pain de mie, *otherwise known as a 'white sandwich loaf', is the bread to use.*

MAKES 2

100 g/3½ oz Gruyère or Emmenthal cheese, grated

4 slices white bread, with the crusts trimmed

2 thick slices ham

1 small egg, beaten

40 g/1½ oz unsalted butter, for frying

for the white sauce

30 g/1 oz unsalted butter

1 tsp sunflower oil

½ tbsp plain flour

125 ml/4 fl oz warm milk

pepper

1 Spread half the grated cheese on 2 slices of bread, then top each with a slice of ham, cut to fit. Sprinkle the ham with all but 2 tablespoons of the remaining cheese, then add the top slices of bread and press down.

2 To make the white sauce, melt the butter with the oil in small heavy-based saucepan over a medium heat. Stir in the flour and stir around for 1 minute to cook out the raw taste. Take the pan off the heat and pour in the milk, stirring constantly. Return the pan to the heat and continue stirring for a minute or so until the sauce is smooth and thickened. Remove the pan from the heat and stir in the remaining cheese and pepper to taste, then set aside and keep warm.

3 Beat the egg in a soup plate or other flat bowl. Add 1 sandwich and press down to coat on both sides, then remove from the bowl and repeat with the other sandwich.

4 Preheat the grill to high. Line a baking tray with foil and set aside. Melt the butter for frying in a sauté or frying pan over a medium-high heat and fry 1 or both sandwiches, depending on the size of your pan, until golden brown on both sides. Add a little extra butter, if necessary, if you have to fry the sandwiches separately.

5 Transfer the sandwiches to the foil-lined baking tray and spread the white sauce over the top. Place under the grill, about 10 cm/4 inches from the heat, and grill for 4 minutes until golden and brown.

variations
When Croque Madame is listed on a menu, it means a fried egg will be added to the ham and cheese filling.

For a more robust flavour, spread the bread with Dijon or wholegrain mustard before adding the ham and cheese.

POULTRY & GAME

74

The French enthusiasm for poultry goes back as far as Henri IV in the late sixteenth century, when he proclaimed: 'I want there to be no peasant in my kingdom so poor that he is unable to have a chicken in his pot every Sunday.'

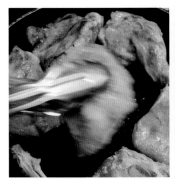 

Volaille is the French word for poultry, including chickens (*poulets*), ducks (*canards*), guinea fowl (*pintades*) and turkeys (*dindes*), which are especially popular at Christmas time. All of these birds are sold at specialist poultry shops (*volaillers*), markets and supermarkets. As the Christmas holidays approach and Christmas markets set up throughout the country, turkeys raised and fattened for the season (*dinde de Noël*) go on sale.

As well as providing fresh birds for cooking at home, most poultry merchants roast whole birds on turning rotisseries, the fat dripping onto potatoes below, ready for chicken-and-potato takeaways. The aromas wafting from the roasting ovens make it difficult to pass without buying.

Wherever one travels in France, restaurant menus are likely to include roast chicken (*poulet rôti*), a dish that is so simple there is nothing to mask a poor roasting technique or an inferior bird. And if you are particularly fortunate, the chicken will come from Bresse, a farming region in the Rhône-Alpes that lies between the Saône River and the foothills of the Jura Mountains to the east. Bresse chickens (*poulets de Bresse*) are an excellent choice for the simple Roast Chicken with Salad (see page 82), but be warned – Bresse chickens are expensive. These corn- and milk-fed, free-range birds are regarded as the undisputed best in France – and there are many who will argue that they are also the best in the world. The French hold Bresse chickens in such high regard that since 1957 the birds have been protected by a coveted Appellation d'Origine Contrôlée (AOC), which was designed to guarantee authenticity and quality, and specifies feed, grazing space and a period of caged 'finishing' before slaughter. The result is a 2 kg/4 lb 8 oz bird with lean white tender flesh covered by a thin layer of fat that adds extra flavour. At a minimum, a Bresse chicken will have roamed free for nine weeks.

If, however, you want to sample one of the other excellent French free-range or corn-fed chickens without the Bresse price tag, look for *poulet fermier* and *poulet de grain*. Organic chickens are labelled as *poulet bio*. Other terms for poultry include *chapon*, a capon (castrated cockerel), *poularde*, a fattened hen, and *poussin*, a young chicken.

Coq au Vin (see page 78) is France's best-known chicken dish. From Burgundy, it has become one of the dishes that typifies French country cooking around the world. Chicken in Riesling (see page 81) from neighbouring Alsace is similar in that the chicken pieces are cooked in wine, but the final dish is very different in flavour and appearance. Try them both to sample distinctly different regional dishes.

An evocative black and white photograph of the Eiffel Tower and the River Seine

Duck recipes often include fruit, as the sharp flavours cut through the richness of the meat

In the south of France, garlic is as much an everyday flavouring as salt and pepper, and it is not for nothing that it is referred to as '*sel de Provence*', or 'salt of Provence', but rarely is it used in such a large quantity as in Chicken with 40 Cloves of Garlic (see page 84). The exact number of garlic cloves isn't important, but several plump heads are needed to make the thick purée served with the thinly sliced meat. As is always said when this traditional recipe is mentioned, even people who claim not to like garlic come back for second helpings of this Provençal dish.

When autumn arrives and temperatures start falling, Guinea Fowl with Cabbage (see page 100) is a comforting country-style dish. Guinea fowl, farmed in northern Provence as well as other parts of France, are lean and the flesh will become dry and unappetizing if not cooked properly. In this slowly cooked casserole, the bird and the Savoy cabbage are oven-cooked with apples and lardons to make a rich and filling dish. Duck meat, on the other hand, can be greasy if not carefully cooked. Roasting a whole duck requires skill, but duck breasts (*magrets*) are easier and quicker to deal with. Duck recipes often include fruit, as the sharp flavours cut through the richness of the meat. Duck Breasts with Fruit Sauce (see page 97) uses summer berries for a sharp sauce that is flavoured with a hint of *quatre-épices*, a typical French spice blend. A subtle use of spices also flavours Rabbit with Prunes (see page 98).

Provence is known for its fields of scented lavender, as well as its herbs, vineyards and olive groves

coq au vin
coq au vin

This rich Burgundian stew was once the farmhouse cook's modest way of tenderizing and flavouring tough old birds. Including cockerel blood, it was not created with modern restaurants in mind, but must now be one of France's best-loved dishes.

SERVES 4–6

1 chicken, weighing 1.6 kg/3 lb 8 oz, cut into 8 pieces

2 tbsp plain flour

85 g/3 oz butter

2 tbsp olive oil

125 g/4¹/₂ oz smoked lardons, blanched for 30 seconds, drained and patted dry

12 shallots, peeled but left whole

4 tbsp brandy

2 large garlic cloves, finely chopped

1 Bouquet Garni

1 tbsp tomato purée

1 tsp caster sugar

1 bottle of dry red wine, such as Beaujolais

12 button mushrooms

salt and pepper

sprigs of fresh flat-leaf parsley, to garnish

Fried Croûtes, to serve

for the beurre manié

15 g/¹/₂ oz butter, softened

15 g/¹/₂ oz plain flour

1 Put the chicken pieces and flour with salt and pepper to taste in a polythene bag, hold the top closed and shake until the chicken pieces are lightly coated all over. Remove the chicken from the bag, shake off any excess flour and set aside.

2 Melt 55 g/2 oz of the butter with 1 tablespoon of the oil in a large sauté or frying pan with a tight-fitting lid or a flameproof casserole over a medium-high heat. Add the lardons and fry for 1 minute. Remove them from the pan with a slotted spoon and set aside.

3 Add the chicken pieces to the pan, skin-side down, and fry for 3–5 minutes until golden brown. Turn the chicken pieces over and continue frying to brown on the other side. Work in batches, if necessary, to avoid overcrowding the pan.

4 Remove the chicken pieces from the pan and set aside. Pour off all but 2 tablespoons of the fat. Add the shallots and sauté them for 3–5 minutes until they are golden on all sides. Transfer to the plate with the lardons and set aside.

5 Return all the chicken pieces to the pan and remove the pan from the heat. Warm the brandy in a ladle or small saucepan, ignite and pour it over the chicken pieces to flambé.

6 When the flames die down, return the pan to the heat, add the garlic, Bouquet Garni, tomato purée, sugar and reserved lardons and shallots and pour in the wine. Bring to the boil, scraping any sediment from the base of the pan.

7 Reduce the heat to low, cover the pan tightly and simmer for 40–45 minutes until the chicken is tender and the juices run clear when a skewer is inserted into the thickest part of the meat.

8 Meanwhile, preheat the oven to its lowest temperature. To make the *beurre manié*, mash the butter and flour together to make a thick paste and set aside.

9 Melt the remaining butter with the remaining oil in another sauté or frying pan over a medium-high heat. Add the mushrooms, season with salt and pepper to taste and sauté them until they are golden. Remove them from the pan and set aside.

10 Remove the chicken pieces from the pan and keep them warm with the mushrooms in the oven. Discard the Bouquet Garni. Tilt the pan and use a large metal spoon to remove the fat from the surface of the cooking liquid, then bring the cooking liquid to the boil and boil for 3 minutes to reduce.

11 Add small amounts of the *beurre manié* to the boiling liquid, whisking constantly and only adding more when the previous amount has been incorporated. Continue boiling and whisking until the sauce is thick and shiny. Taste, and adjust the seasoning if necessary. Spoon the sauce over the chicken pieces and mushrooms. Garnish with parsley sprigs and serve immediately with the Fried Croûtes.

chicken in riesling

poulet au riesling

*This is Alsace's answer to Burgundy's Coq au Vin –
an equally traditional rich chicken cooked with wine,
although this version is further enriched with cream.*

SERVES 4–6

1 chicken, weighing 1.6 kg/3 lb 8 oz, cut into 8 pieces,
  or 8 chicken thighs

2 tbsp plain flour

55 g/2 oz unsalted butter

1 tbsp sunflower oil

4 shallots, finely chopped

12 button mushrooms, sliced

2 tbsp brandy

500 ml/18 fl oz Riesling wine

250 ml/9 fl oz double cream

salt and pepper

chopped fresh flat-leaf parsley, to serve

1 Put the chicken pieces and flour with salt and
pepper to taste in a polythene bag, hold the top
closed and shake until the chicken pieces are lightly
coated all over. Remove the chicken from the bag, shake
off any excess flour and set aside.

2 Melt 30 g/1 oz of the butter with the oil in a large
sauté pan or frying pan with a tight-fitting lid or
a flameproof casserole over a medium-high heat. Add
the chicken pieces to the pan, skin-side down, and fry
for 3–5 minutes until golden brown. Turn the chicken
pieces over and continue frying to brown on the other
side. Work in batches, if necessary, to avoid
overcrowding the pan.

3 Remove the chicken pieces from the pan and set
aside. Pour off all the fat in the pan and wipe the
pan with kitchen paper. Melt the remaining butter in
the pan over a medium-high heat. When the butter
stops foaming, add the shallots and mushrooms to the
pan and sauté them, stirring constantly, for 3 minutes,
or until the shallots are golden and the mushrooms are
lightly browned.

4 Return all the chicken pieces to the pan and remove
the pan from the heat. Warm the brandy in a ladle
or small saucepan, ignite and pour it over the chicken
pieces to flambé.

5 When the flames die down, return the pan to the
heat, pour in the wine and slowly bring to the boil,
scraping any sediment from the base of the pan. Reduce
the heat to low, cover the pan tightly and simmer for
40–45 minutes until the chicken is tender and the juices
run clear when a skewer is inserted into the thickest
part of the meat.

6 Meanwhile, preheat the oven to its lowest
temperature. Remove the chicken pieces from the
pan, transfer them to a large serving platter and keep
them warm in the oven.

7 Tilt the pan and use a large metal spoon to remove
the fat from the surface of the cooking liquid. Stir
in the cream and bring the sauce to the boil. The sauce
will boil quickly and should reduce by half almost
instantly. Add salt and pepper to taste.

8 To serve, spoon the sauce with the mushrooms and
shallots over the chicken pieces and sprinkle with
the parsley.

82 roast chicken with salad
poulet rôti avec salade

French cooks do not normally thicken roasting juices with flour or cornflour to make gravy. Instead, they deglaze the roasting tin with wine or stock to make thin, flavoursome juice, or jus, to be spooned over the carved chicken. In the recipe, the cooking juices also flavour a salad dressing to serve with the chicken or as a separate, following course, perhaps in place of dessert.

SERVES 4–6

1 chicken, weighing 1.7 kg/3 lb 12 oz, rinsed inside
  and out and dried
1 garlic clove, crushed
1 sprig of fresh thyme
1 large sprig of fresh flat-leaf parsley
finely grated rind of 1 lemon
85 g/3 oz unsalted butter, softened
2 tbsp very finely chopped fresh flat-leaf parsley
2 tbsp very finely chopped fresh chervil
250 ml/9 fl oz Chicken Stock or dry white or red wine
salt and pepper
fresh watercress leaves, to garnish

for the salad
2–3 tbsp Garlic Vinaigrette
225–300 g/8–10¹/₂ oz mixed salad leaves

1 Preheat the oven to 190°C/375°F/Gas Mark 5. Weigh the chicken and calculate the exact roasting time at 20 minutes per 500 g/1 lb 2 oz, plus 20 minutes.

2 Put the garlic, thyme, parsley sprig, lemon rind, 30 g/1 oz of the butter and a generous seasoning of the salt and pepper inside the chicken, then truss to tie the legs together. Mash the remaining butter with a fork, then work in the chopped parsley and chervil and add salt and pepper to taste. Use your fingers to smear the herb butter all over the chicken breasts.

3 Lay the chicken on one side on a rack in a roasting tin not much larger than the bird. Transfer to the oven and roast for 20 minutes, then turn the chicken onto its other side and spoon the roasting juices over.

4 After another 20 minutes, turn the chicken breast-side up, baste again and continue roasting for a further 50 minutes, basting every 15 minutes or so, or until the chicken is tender and the juices run clear when a skewer is inserted into the thickest part of the meat.

5 Tip the cavity juices into the roasting tin. Set the chicken aside on a serving platter, cover loosely with foil and leave to rest for 10 minutes before carving.

6 Meanwhile, tilt the roasting tin and use a large metal spoon to remove the fat from the surface of the juices. Remove about 1 tablespoon of the cooking juices and set aside to use in the salad dressing.

7 Place the roasting tin over a medium-high heat and deglaze it by stirring in the stock and scraping loose any sediment from the base of the tin with a wooden spoon. Bring to the boil and continue boiling until the juices reduce slightly. Taste, and adjust the seasoning if necessary.

8 Thinly slice the chicken, spoon the juices over and garnish with the watercress leaves. When you are ready to eat, prepare the salad by stirring the reserved cooking juices into the Garlic Vinaigrette and adjusting the seasoning, if necessary. Put the leaves in a bowl, add the Vinaigrette and toss together. Serve with the chicken.

84

chicken with 40 cloves of garlic
poulet aux 40 gousses d'ail

One of the almost magical properties of garlic is that its pungent raw cloves become meltingly tender and mild-tasting after gentle, slow cooking, which is what makes this traditional casserole from Vaucluse so popular. In summer months, this is ideal to serve with a bottle of chilled rosé wine.

SERVES 4–6

1 chicken, weighing 1.7 kg/3 lb 12 oz, rinsed inside
  and out and dried

4 tbsp olive oil

40 garlic cloves, unpeeled

2 sprigs of fresh thyme

2 sprigs of fresh flat-leaf parsley

1 bay leaf

200 ml/7 fl oz Vegetable Stock or hot water

salt and pepper

chopped fresh flat-leaf parsley, to garnish

Another Parisian icon, the Notre Dame cathedral, lies on the Ile de la Cité in the middle of the Seine

1 Truss the chicken to tie the legs together. Heat the oil in a large flameproof casserole over a medium-high heat. Add the chicken and fry on 1 side until golden, then turn over and fry on the other side until golden. Remove the chicken from the casserole and set aside.

2 Put the garlic in the casserole, then top with the thyme and parsley sprigs and the bay leaf. Put the chicken on top, breast-side up, and rub with salt and pepper. Cover the casserole and place over a low heat for 1½ hours, or until the meat is tender and the juices run clear when a skewer is inserted into the thickest part of the meat.

3 Transfer the chicken to a warmed serving platter, cover with foil, shiny-side down, and set aside.

4 Place a fine sieve over a bowl and tip in the garlic cloves, herbs and cooking juices from the casserole, discarding the bay leaf. Use a wooden spoon to press the soft garlic cloves and herbs through the sieve to make a coarse purée.

5 Return the casserole to a medium-high heat. Pour in the stock and bring to the boil, scraping any sediment from the base of the pan. Stir in the garlic purée, then taste and adjust the seasoning.

6 Slice the chicken and serve with the garlic juices spooned over and garnished with the parsley.*

*cook's tip
Another way to present this dish is to cut the chicken into portions and serve with the whole cooked garlic cloves. Each diner uses a fork to squeeze the soft cloves on the side of their plate and then spreads the purée onto the chicken portions.

88 chicken in tarragon sauce
poulet sauce estragon

Chicken and tarragon are a classic flavour combination. The silvery-green herb with a slightly aniseed flavour grows well in Provence and it is often included in French egg and potato dishes as well as chicken recipes such as this rich summer dish. Tarragon is one herb that should always be used fresh, as dried it has little flavour, but use it judiciously – the flavour can easily overpower. Tarragon is also one of the herbs included in the classic French mixture fines herbes.

SERVES 4

4 boneless chicken breasts, about 175 g/6 oz each

30 g/1 oz unsalted butter

1 tbsp sunflower oil

salt and pepper*

for the Tarragon Sauce

2 tbsp tarragon-flavoured vinegar

6 tbsp dry white wine, such as Muscadet

250 ml/9 fl oz Chicken Stock

4 sprigs of fresh tarragon, plus 2 tbsp chopped
   fresh tarragon

300 ml/10 fl oz crème fraîche or double cream

1 Preheat the oven to 190°C/375°F/Gas Mark 5. Season the chicken breasts on both sides with salt and pepper.

2 Melt the butter with the oil in a sauté or frying pan, large enough to hold the chicken pieces in a single layer, over a medium-high heat. Add the chicken breasts, skin-side down, and fry for 3–5 minutes until golden brown.

3 Transfer the chicken breasts to a roasting tin and roast for 15–20 minutes, or until they are tender and the juices run clear when a skewer is inserted into the thickest part of the meat. Transfer the chicken to a serving platter, cover with foil, shiny-side down, and set aside.

4 To make the Tarragon Sauce, tilt the roasting tin and use a large metal spoon to remove the excess fat from the surface of the cooking juices. Place the roasting tin over a medium-high heat and add the vinegar, scraping any sediment from the base of the tin. Pour in the wine and bring to the boil, still stirring and scraping, and boil until the liquid is reduced by half.

5 Stir in the stock and whole tarragon sprigs and continue boiling until the liquid reduces to about 125 ml/4 fl oz.

6 Stir in the crème fraîche and continue boiling to reduce all the liquid by half. Discard the tarragon sprigs, and adjust the seasoning if necessary. Stir the chopped tarragon into the sauce.

7 To serve, slice the chicken breasts on individual plates and spoon a quarter of the sauce over each.

*cook's tip
For a refined sauce without black flecks, use ground white pepper, rather than black.

Overleaf Thousands of acres of sunflowers are grown in France for the cooking oil 'huile de tournesol'

old-fashioned roast chicken
poulet grand-mère

Whenever the description grand-mère *appears in a French recipe title, expect to find lardons, button mushrooms, small onions and potatoes in the dish. This is a one-pot dish that doesn't need any other accompaniment. It's a homely, comforting supper dish – just like grandmother used to make.*

SERVES 4

1 chicken, weighing 1.5 kg/3 lb 5 oz, rinsed inside
  and out and dried

55 g/2 oz unsalted butter

1 large onion, quartered

3 tbsp sunflower oil

350 g/12 oz waxy potatoes, such as Charlotte,
  peeled and diced

250 g/9 oz smoked lardons

250 g/9 oz pickling onions, peeled but left whole

250 g/9 oz button mushrooms

250 ml/9 fl oz Chicken Stock

salt and pepper

chopped fresh flat-leaf parsley, to garnish

1 Preheat the oven to 190°C/375°F/Gas Mark 5. Weigh the chicken and calculate the exact roasting time at 20 minutes per 500 g/1 lb 2 oz, plus 20 minutes. Melt 40 g/1½ oz of the butter and set aside.

2 Season the chicken inside and out to taste with salt and pepper and put the onion quarters in the cavity, then truss to tie the legs together. Place the chicken in a roasting tin over a medium heat with 1 tablespoon of the oil and the melted butter. Fry the chicken for 15 minutes, or until it is golden brown all over. Remove the chicken from the pan and pour off the excess fat.

3 Place a rack inside the roasting tin, put the chicken on it on one of its sides and transfer to the oven. Roast the chicken for 15 minutes, then turn it onto its other side and continue roasting for another 15 minutes.

4 Meanwhile, put the potatoes in a saucepan, cover with cold salted water and boil for 2 minutes. Drain the potatoes well and pat them dry with a tea towel.

5 Heat 1 tablespoon of the remaining oil in a large sauté or frying pan over a medium-high heat. Add the lardons and pickling onions and fry, stirring occasionally, for 5 minutes, or until the onions are golden all over. Remove the lardons and onions from the pan and set aside.

6 Melt the remaining butter into the fat remaining in the pan. Add the mushrooms and sauté until they are golden.

7 After the chicken has been roasting for 30 minutes, remove the tin from the oven. Removing the rack, position the chicken breast-side up, spoon the cooking juices over the breast and sprinkle with salt and pepper. Arrange the potatoes, mushrooms, onions and lardons around the chicken, then return to the oven to continue roasting for a further 30 minutes, or until the chicken is tender and the juices run clear when a skewer is inserted into the thickest part of the meat.

8 When the chicken is cooked through, reduce the oven temperature to its lowest setting, transfer the vegetables and lardons to an ovenproof bowl and put in the oven to keep warm. Untie the trussing strings and tip the cavity juices into the roasting tin. Transfer the chicken to a serving platter, cover loosely with foil and leave to rest for 10 minutes before carving.

9 Tilt the roasting tin and use a large metal spoon to remove the excess fat from the surface of the cooking juices. Place the tin over a medium-high heat and add the stock, scraping any sediment from the base of the tin. Bring to the boil and continue boiling until the juices reduce. Stir in any juices from the platter with the chicken, then taste, and adjust the seasoning if necessary.

10 Cut the chicken into serving portions. Sprinkle the vegetables and lardons with parsley and serve with the chicken. Serve the juices on the side for spooning over.

94 chicken and almond tagine
tagine de poulet aux amandes

This fragrant North African-style stew, coloured with saffron and flavoured with a hint of chilli, is a legacy of France's colonial past. Chicken is the main ingredient in this version, but seafood, meat and vegetables are also given the tagine treatment in any neighbourhood with a North African immigrant community. With a mix of spicy, sweet and savoury flavours in a pot, a tagine served with couscous provides a light alternative to more traditional French food.

SERVES 4–6

large pinch of saffron threads

3 tbsp olive or sunflower oil

2 large onions, sliced

1 chicken, weighing 1.7 kg/3 lb 12 oz, cut into 8 pieces, or 8 large thighs

500 ml/18 fl oz water

1 bouquet garni of 4 sprigs of fresh parsley, 4 sprigs of fresh coriander and 1 bay leaf, tied together

1 large garlic clove, crushed

1 tbsp ground ginger

¹/₂ tsp dried chilli flakes

125 g/4¹/₂ oz ready-to-eat dried apricots

100 g/3¹/₂ oz whole blanched almonds

1 preserved lemon, sliced

salt and pepper

chopped fresh coriander, to garnish

1 lemon, cut into quarters, to serve (optional)

1 Put the saffron threads in a small dry frying pan over a high heat and toast, stirring constantly, for 1 minute, or until you can smell the aroma. Immediately tip the saffron threads out of the pan and set aside.

2 Heat the oil in a flameproof casserole over a medium-high heat. Add the onions and fry, stirring frequently, for 5–8 minutes until golden, but not brown. Remove the onions from the pan with a slotted spoon and set aside.

3 Add the chicken pieces to the casserole, skin-side down, and fry for 3–5 minutes until golden brown. Turn the chicken pieces over and continue frying to brown on the other side, adding a little extra oil, if necessary. Work in batches to avoid overcrowding the pan.

4 Pour off any excess fat in the casserole, then return all the chicken pieces to the pan. Pour over enough water to cover by at least 2.5 cm/1 inch and slowly bring to the boil, skimming the surface as necessary. When the foam stops rising to the surface, stir in the onions, saffron threads, bouquet garni, garlic, ginger, chilli flakes and salt and pepper to taste.

5 Cover the casserole and leave the tagine to simmer for 30 minutes, then check the seasoning of the cooking liquid and add more ginger, chilli flakes or salt and pepper, if necessary. Stir in the apricots and continue simmering for 15–30 minutes, or until the chicken pieces are tender and the juices run clear when a skewer is inserted into a thick piece of meat.

6 Meanwhile, transfer a ladleful of the cooking liquid to a small saucepan, add the almonds and simmer for 10 minutes, or until tender. Drain well and set aside.

7 Transfer the chicken pieces to a deep serving platter and scatter the almonds and preserved lemon over. Bring the cooking liquid to the boil and boil to reduce by half. Discard the bouquet garni, then pour the cooking liquid over the chicken pieces. Sprinkle with chopped coriander and serve with lemon wedges for squeezing over.*

*cook's tip

Freshly cooked couscous is the ideal accompaniment to this dish. The authentic method for cooking couscous is to steam it above the simmering tagine. However, quick-cooking couscous, sold in supermarkets, is a simpler, quicker alternative. To prepare quick-cooking couscous, put 70 g/2½ oz quick-cooking couscous grains per person in a heatproof bowl with a knob of butter and salt and pepper, to taste. Pour over enough boiling water or Vegetable Stock to cover the grains by about 1 cm/½ inch, then cover the bowl with a folded tea towel and leave to stand for 5 minutes, or until all the liquid is absorbed and the grains are tender. Stir well, and adjust the seasoning if necessary.

variation

The dried apricots can be replaced with dried figs or dates. Sultanas or raisins are also good stirred into the tagine mixture in Step 5.

duck breasts with fruit sauce
magrets sauce aux fruits

Quickly cooked duck breasts are often served with a fruit sauce to cut through the richness of the meat. Duck and orange is a popular combination, but here mixed fresh or frozen summer fruits with just a small hint of spice are used in this quick and easy sauce. On the plate, this simple dish looks as if it has been prepared in a stylish French restaurant.

SERVES 4

4 boneless duck breasts, about 175 g/6 oz each

1 tbsp sunflower oil

125 ml/4 fl oz dry white wine

125 g/4¹/₂ oz frozen mixed berries, straight from the freezer, or fresh berries

1 tbsp clear honey

¹/₄ tsp quatre–épices or ground mixed spice

salt and pepper

1 Preheat the oven to 200°C/400°F/Gas Mark 6. Finely score each duck breast in a criss-cross pattern through the skin into the fat.*

2 Heat the oil in a large sauté or frying pan over a high heat. Add the duck breasts, skin-side down, and fry for 4 minutes, or until the skin is golden brown. Transfer the duck breasts to a roasting tin, skin-side up, and roast for 12 minutes for medium-rare, or 15 minutes for medium.

3 Meanwhile, tip the excess fat out of the sauté pan. Place the pan over a high heat, add the wine and bring to the boil, scraping any sediment from the base of the pan with a wooden spoon. Stir in the fruit, reduce the heat to medium and leave to simmer for 5 minutes, or until tender, stirring occasionally and pressing down with the back of a wooden spoon.

4 Stir in the honey and spice until the honey dissolves. Season to taste with salt and pepper and add extra honey or spice, as desired. Reduce the heat to low and leave the sauce to simmer and reduce, stirring occasionally.

5 Transfer the duck breasts to a carving board, cover with foil and leave to stand for a few minutes. Thinly slice the duck breasts on the diagonal and transfer to serving plates. Add any accumulated duck juices to the sauce, and adjust the seasoning if necessary.

6 At this point, the sauce can be used as it is with pieces of fruit or puréed in a food processor or blender and passed through a non-metallic sieve for a smooth sauce, reheating if necessary. Spoon the fruit sauce over the duck breasts and serve.

*cook's tip
Thinly scoring the skin of the duck breasts helps to render the fat during the initial cooking in Step 2. The rendered fat is excellent for sautéeing potatoes, so it is worth pouring it into a heatproof bowl and leaving to cool completely. Then it can be covered and stored in the refrigerator for several weeks.

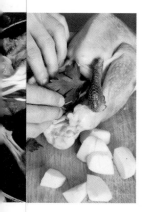

100 guinea fowl with cabbage
pintade au chou

1 Preheat the oven to 240°C/475°F/Gas Mark 9. Rub the guinea fowl with the oil and season to taste inside and out with salt and pepper. Put the apple and parsley sprigs in the guinea fowl's cavity and truss to tie the legs together. Place the guinea fowl in a roasting tin and roast for 20 minutes to colour the breasts. When the guinea fowl is golden brown, immediately reduce the oven temperature to 160°C/325°F/Gas Mark 3.

2 Meanwhile, bring a large saucepan of salted water to the boil. Add the cabbage and blanch for 3 minutes. Drain, rinse in cold water and pat dry.

3 Place the lardons in a flameproof casserole over a medium-high heat and sauté until they give off their fat. Use a slotted spoon to remove the lardons from the casserole and set aside.

4 Add the onion to the fat left in the casserole and cook, stirring frequently, for 5 minutes, or until the onion is tender, but not brown. Stir the Bouquet Garni into the pan with a very little salt and a pinch of pepper, then return the lardons to the pan.*

5 Add the cabbage to the casserole, top with the guinea fowl and cover the whole surface with a piece of wet greaseproof paper. Then cover the casserole and put it in the oven for 45–60 minutes, or until the guinea fowl is tender and the juices run clear when a skewer is inserted into the thickest part of the meat.

6 Remove the guinea fowl from the casserole and cut into serving portions. Discard the Bouquet Garni, then stir the parsley into the cabbage and onion, then taste, and adjust the seasoning if necessary. Serve the guinea fowl portions on a bed of cabbage and onion.

Rich and opulent, the height of French baroque finds a parallel in many of the country's finest dishes

This is a comforting winter dish. The cabbage reduces in the bacon-flavoured cooking juices to make a thick 'sauce' to serve the guinea fowl on.

SERVES 4

1 guinea fowl, weighing 1.25 kg/2 lb 12 oz, oven-ready

¹/₂ tbsp sunflower oil

¹/₂ apple, peeled, cored and chopped

several sprigs of fresh flat-leaf parsley, stems bruised

1 large Savoy cabbage, coarse outer leaves removed, cored and quartered

1 thick piece of smoked belly of pork, about 140 g/5 oz, rind removed and cut into thin lardons, or 140 g/5 oz unsmoked lardons

1 onion, sliced

1 Bouquet Garni

1¹/₂ tbsp chopped fresh flat-leaf parsley

salt and pepper

*cook's tip

It is important not to add too much salt in Step 4 as the lardons will be salty.

MEAT

104 The French are great meat-eaters as any vegetarian travelling through France will testify. The importance the French attach to meat in their diet is evident in the fact that the French word for meat, *viande*, once meant 'food'. However, the French tend to eat meat frequently, but rarely in huge quantities.

Butchers (*boucheries*) provide beef (*boeuf*), lamb (*agneau*), pork (*porc*) and veal (*veau*), while a *boucherie chevaline* is the place to go to buy horse meat (*viande de cheval*), a French favourite, cooked like beef. These shops are often sited next to more conventional butchers, but are easily recognizable by the horse head on a sign or above the door.

Steak and chips (*steak et frites*) is thought of as typically French, but French author Alexandre Dumas, writing in 1870, credits the English with introducing beef steaks to France. 'I saw the birth of the *bifteck* [beef steak] in Paris after the three-year occupation by the English in 1815... since we are an eclectic and unprejudiced people, we soon perceived that, although the Greeks bore this gift, it was not poisoned, and we handed the *bifteck* its certificate of citizenship,' he wrote in his *Grand Dictionnaire de Cuisine*, published posthumously in 1873.

Cattle are raised in many regions of France, such as in Limousin and in the Gironde region near Bordeaux, but it is the free-range, white-haired Charolais breed from Burgundy that is the most sought after for its flavoursome, tender, low-fat meat. This is reflected in its price in France and abroad: as in other countries, the best-quality French meat is expensive, so the rule of thumb among chefs when dealing with a prime cuts is that less is more. Pepper Steak (see page 114) illustrates the quick-frying technique favoured for steaks and chops. Sautéed Potatoes (see page 183) are the ideal accompaniment. Other recipes for quickly cooked, top-quality meat include Steak with Parsley Butter (see page 110) and Veal Chops with Wild Mushroom Sauce (see page 133).

Less prime cuts are slowly simmered with vegetables, wine and stock until meltingly tender. All French kitchens include at least one well-used cast-iron casserole in which the ingredients for stews are quickly fried on the hob before being transferred to the oven for slow cooking. Beef stews are a testimony to French culinary ingenuity. All over the country the same basic ingredients of beef and wine are combined with vegetables and transformed into unique dishes. Beef Bourguignon (see page 108), with

Situated in the heart of the Latin Quarter, the Notre Dame is one of Paris's most imposing Gothic cathedrals

its full-bodied red wine, mushrooms and small onions, has come to symbolize French beef stews around the world, but it is only one of many. Beef Stew with Olives (see page 112), from Provence, is given a typical local twist with black olives and a hint of orange. In Alsace, *baekenofe*, which translates as 'baker's oven', is a combination of beef, pork and lamb with a local white wine. Its name reflects back to when Monday was the washing day and busy housewives took casseroles filled with meat and vegetables to the local bakery for cooking in the wood-fired ovens after bread baking was finished. In northern France, beer replaces wine to make a traditional beef stew called *carbonade*. Other meal-in-a-pot stews in this chapter include Spring Lamb Stew (see page 118) and Veal with Mushrooms in a Cream Sauce (see page 134). Cassoulet (see page 129), from southwestern France, is a hearty bean casserole that can include chicken, duck, goose, lamb and pork, or any combination, with many, many variations.

Along with Charolais beef from Burgundy, French meat-eaters are also blessed with lambs that graze on salt marshes along the Atlantic coast and the English Channel to achieve a distinctively salty flavour that commands a high price in markets. Even if *agneau pre-salé*, as the salty lamb from Normandy and Brittany is called, isn't available, try Roast Lamb with Beans (see page 117) for the typically French combination of lamb and flageolet beans.

Offal (*abats*) is also treated with respect throughout France. Tripe, for example, might have only limited fans in other countries, but *tripes à la mode de Caen* from Normandy is considered a delicacy, combined with Calvados or cider. Kidneys in Mustard Sauce (see page 115) is an offal speciality from Dijon, the country's mustard capital.

The Arc de Triomphe assumes pride of place among the monuments of Paris, as exciting by night as it is by day

108

beef bourguignon
boeuf à la bourguignonne

Of all the beef stews in France, this one from the famed wine-producing region of Burgundy is probably the best known. Custom dictates that the wine used in cooking is also served with the meal.

SERVES 4–6

85 g/3 oz butter

2 tbsp sunflower oil

175 g/6 oz smoked lardons, blanched for 30 seconds, drained and patted dry

900 g/2 lb stewing beef, such as chuck or leg, trimmed and cut into 5-cm/2-inch chunks

2 large garlic cloves, crushed

1 carrot, peeled and diced

1 leek, halved, rinsed and sliced

1 onion, finely chopped

2 tbsp plain flour

350 ml/12 fl oz full-bodied red Burgundy wine, such as Hermitage or Côtes du Rhône

about 500 ml/18 fl oz beef stock

1 tbsp tomato purée

1 Bouquet Garni

12 pickling onions, peeled but left whole

12 button mushrooms

salt and pepper

chopped fresh flat-leaf parsley, to garnish

French bread, to serve

1 Preheat the oven to 150°C/300°F/Gas Mark 2. Melt 30 g/1 oz of the butter with 1 tablespoon of the oil in a large flameproof casserole over a medium-high heat. Add the lardons and fry for 2 minutes, or until they start to brown, then drain on kitchen paper.

2 Fry the beef in the fat remaining in the casserole until brown on all sides, working in batches, if necessary, to avoid overcrowding the casserole. Add extra butter or oil to the casserole as necessary. Transfer the beef cubes to a plate as they brown, to catch the juices, and set aside.

3 Pour off all but 2 tablespoons of the fat from the casserole. Add the garlic, carrot, leek and onion and sauté for 3 minutes, or until the onion is starting to soften. Sprinkle in the flour with salt and pepper to taste and continue sautéeing for a further 2 minutes.

4 Stir in the wine, stock, tomato purée and the Bouquet Garni and bring to the boil, scraping the sediment from the base of the casserole. Return the beef and lardons to the casserole and pour in extra stock, if necessary, so that the ingredients are covered by about 1 cm/½ inch.

5 Slowly return the casserole to the boil, then cover the casserole and place it in the oven to cook for 2 hours.

6 Meanwhile, melt 30 g/1 oz of the remaining butter with the remaining oil in a large sauté or frying pan over a medium-high heat. Add the pickling onions to the pan and sauté them, stirring frequently, until golden on all sides. Use a slotted spoon to remove the onions from the pan and set aside.

7 Melt the remaining butter in the pan. Add the mushrooms and season them to taste with salt and pepper, then sauté, stirring, until they are golden. Remove from the pan and set aside.

8 After the casserole has cooked for 2 hours, stir in the sautéed onions and mushrooms. Re-cover the casserole and continue simmering in the oven for 30 minutes, or until the beef is very tender.

9 Discard the Bouquet Garni. Taste, and adjust the seasoning if necessary. Sprinkle over the parsley and serve with plenty of French bread for mopping up all the juices.*

cook's tip

Like most stews, this tastes best made a day in advance and reheated. To do this, remove the casserole from the oven after 1½ hours' simmering. The next day, add the mushrooms and onions and slowly bring to the boil on the hob, then place in the preheated oven and cook for 30–45 minutes until the beef is tender.

110 # steak with parsley butter
entrecôte beurre maître d'hôtel

Entrecôte *translates as 'between the ribs', which is where the tender steaks that the French like grilled or quickly pan-fried come from. Entrecôte, however, is a cut not readily available outside France, but sirloin or rib-eye steaks are similar. The savoury herb butter in this recipe can be prepared well in advance and frozen, then used straight from the freezer to make this a very quick meal.*

SERVES 2

30 g/1 oz butter

1 tbsp sunflower oil

2 sirloin or rib-eye steaks, about 175 g/6 oz each
  and 2 cm/³/₄ inch thick, at room temperature

salt and pepper

for the Parsley Butter

55 g/2 oz unsalted butter, softened

1¹/₂ tbsp very finely chopped fresh flat-leaf parsley

squeeze of lemon juice

salt

cayenne pepper

1 To make the Parsley Butter, put the butter in a small bowl and beat until it is smooth. Add the parsley and lemon juice with salt and cayenne pepper to taste and beat again until combined. Spoon the butter onto a piece of greaseproof paper and roll it into a sausage shape about 2.5 cm/1 inch thick. Chill in the refrigerator for 2 hours, or until firm, or freeze for up to a month.

2 When you are ready to cook the steaks, melt the butter and oil in a large sauté or frying pan over a medium-high heat. Cook the steaks for 1 minute on each side to brown. Reduce the heat to medium, season the steaks to taste with salt and pepper and continue cooking for a further 2–3 minutes for rare; 4–5 minutes for medium; and 6–8 minutes for well done.

3 Transfer the steaks to warmed serving plates and spoon over the cooking juices from the pan. Cut the parsley butter into 6 thin slices and top each steak with 3 slices. Serve at once.

variations

French cooks often use savoury butters, like the one above, as a quick way to add extra flavour to simply pan-fried or grilled chops or steaks. Try these variations, each of which should be made with 100 g/3¹/₂ oz softened unsalted butter and salt and pepper to taste to make 4–6 portions:

Anchovy Butter (*Beurre d'anchois*) Beat in 6 drained and mashed anchovy fillets with 2 teaspoons chopped fresh parsley or tarragon.

Garlic Butter (*Beurre d'ail*) Beat in 2 peeled and crushed garlic cloves.

Horseradish Butter (*Beurre de raifort*) Stir in 2 tablespoons creamed horseradish.

Mustard Butter (*Beurre de moutarde*) Stir in 2 tablespoons Dijon or wholegrain mustard with 2 teaspoons chopped fresh parsley or tarragon.

112 beef stew with olives
boeuf en daube à la provençale

This stew gets its name from a daubière, *the traditional Provençal earthenware pot it is cooked in. In Provence, this is often served with buttered noodles, but a mound of hot mashed potatoes also makes an ideal accompaniment. For a two-course meal in a pot Provençal-style, serve the flavoursome juices in a soup bowl with the noodles as a first course, then the meat and vegetables as a second course.*

SERVES 4–6

900 g/2 lb stewing beef, such as chuck or leg, trimmed
   and cut into 5-cm/2-inch chunks

2 onions, thinly sliced

2 carrots, thickly sliced

4 large garlic cloves, bruised

1 large bouquet garni of 2 sprigs of fresh flat-leaf
   parsley, 2 sprigs of fresh thyme and 2 bay leaves, tied
   to a piece of celery

4 juniper berries

500 ml/18 fl oz full-bodied dry red wine, such as Fitou

2 tbsp brandy

2 tbsp olive oil

225 g/8 oz boned belly of pork, rind removed

200 g/7 oz plain flour

2 x 10-cm/4-inch strips of orange rind

85 g/3 oz black olives, stoned and rinsed to remove
  any brine

beef stock, if necessary

90 ml/3 fl oz water

salt and pepper

to garnish

chopped fresh flat-leaf parsley

finely grated orange rind

1 Put the beef in a large glass or earthenware bowl and add the onions, carrots, garlic, bouquet garni, juniper berries and salt and pepper to taste. Pour over the wine, brandy and oil and give a good stir. Cover with clingfilm and marinate in the refrigerator for 24 hours.

2 Remove the beef and marinade from the refrigerator 30 minutes before you plan to cook, and preheat the oven to 160°C/325°F/Gas Mark 3. Meanwhile, cut the belly of pork into 5-mm/¼-inch strips. Bring a saucepan of water to the boil and add the pork. Return to the boil and blanch for 3 minutes, then drain.

3 Remove the beef from the marinade and pat dry with kitchen paper. Put the beef and 3 tablespoons of the flour with salt and pepper in a polythene bag, hold the top closed and shake until the beef chunks are lightly coated all over. Remove the beef from the bag, shake off any excess flour and set aside.

4 Transfer half the pork slices to a 3.4-litre/6-pint flameproof casserole. Top with the beef and marinade, including the vegetables and bouquet garni, and add the orange rind and olives. Scatter the remaining pork slices over. If the wine doesn't cover all the ingredients, top up with beef stock.

5 Mix the remaining flour with the water to form a thick, pliable paste. Slowly bring the casserole to the boil on top of the hob, then put the lid on the casserole and use your fingers to press the paste around the sides

to form a tight seal. Transfer the casserole to the oven and cook for 1 hour. Reduce the oven temperature to 140°C/275°F/Gas Mark 1 and continue cooking for a further 3 hours.

6 Remove the casserole from the oven and use a serrated knife to cut off the seal. Use the tip of the knife to ensure that the beef and carrots are tender. If not, re-cover the casserole and return it to the oven, testing again after 15 minutes.

7 Using a large metal spoon, skim any fat from the surface and adjust the seasoning if necessary. Remove the bouquet garni, sprinkle the parsley and orange rind over the top, and serve. Alternatively, leave to cool completely, cover and chill overnight. Before reheating, scrape the solid fat off the surface.

variation
As an alternative to the belly of pork, you could use 125 g/4½ oz unsmoked lardons.

114

pepper steak
steak au poivre

SERVES 4

2 tbsp black or mixed dried peppercorns, coarsely
   crushed*

4 fillets steaks, about 2.5 cm/1 inch thick, at room
   temperature

15 g/¹/₂ oz butter

1 tsp sunflower oil

4 tbsp brandy

4 tbsp crème fraîche or double cream (optional)

salt and pepper

watercress leaves, to garnish

*Lean, tender fillet steaks are usually used for this
popular bistro-style dish, but slightly less expensive
sirloin steaks are also suitable. Some chefs make the
robust sauce simply by deglazing the cooking pan
with brandy, while others add and reduce crème
fraîche or double cream for an even richer sauce.
The choice is yours.*

1 Spread out the crushed peppercorns on a plate and
press the steaks into them to coat on both sides.

2 Melt the butter with the oil in a large sauté or
frying pan over a medium-high heat. Add the
steaks in a single layer and cook for 3 minutes on each
side for rare; 3¹/₂ minutes on each side for medium-rare;
4 minutes on each side for medium; and 4¹/₂–5 minutes
on each side for well done.

3 Transfer the steaks to a warmed plate and set aside,
covering with foil to keep warm. Pour the brandy
into the pan to deglaze, increase the heat and use a
wooden spoon to scrape any sediment from the base of
the pan. Continue boiling until reduced to around
2 tablespoons.

4 Stir in any accumulated juices from the steaks.
Spoon in the crème fraîche, if using, and continue
boiling until the sauce is reduced by half again. Taste,
and adjust the seasoning if necessary. Spoon the pan
sauce over the steaks, garnish with the watercress and
serve at once.

*cook's tip

To crush the peppercorns coarsely, put them in a thick
polythene bag and bash with a rolling pin. Alternatively,
use a pestle and mortar, but take care not to grind
them too finely.

kidneys in mustard sauce
rognons sauce moutarde

Burgundy is known throughout the world for its fine wines, but Dijon, the ancient capital city, is also the mustard capital of France. The yellow, smooth Dijon mustard is used to flavour poultry, meat, fish and offal dishes, as well as being a condiment. This dish appears on many bistro menus.

SERVES 4–6

12 lamb's kidneys, skinned and halved

30 g/1 oz unsalted butter

1 tbsp sunflower oil

2 large shallots, chopped

1 garlic clove, very finely chopped

2 tbsp dry white wine

125 ml/4 fl oz Chicken Stock or lamb stock

250 ml/9 oz double cream

2 tbsp Dijon mustard, or to taste

salt and pepper

chopped fresh flat-leaf parsley, to garnish

1 Use a pair of kitchen scissors to remove the kidney cores. Melt the butter with the oil in a large sauté or frying pan over a medium-high heat. Add the kidney halves and fry, turning occasionally, for 3 minutes, or until brown all over, working in batches, if necessary, to avoid overcrowding the pan. Use a slotted spoon to transfer the kidney halves to a plate, then cover with foil, shiny-side down, set aside and keep warm.

2 Add the shallots and garlic to the fat in the pan and sauté for 2 minutes, or until the shallots are soft, but not coloured. Add the wine and boil until it reduces by half, scraping the sediment from the base of the pan.

3 Add the stock and boil again until reduced by half. Stir in the cream and mustard, reduce the heat to medium-low and return the kidneys to the pan. Cover and simmer for 5 minutes, or until the kidneys are cooked through.

4 Remove the kidneys from the pan and keep warm. Increase the heat under the sauce and leave it to bubble until it reduces and thickens. Add salt and pepper to taste, return the kidneys and stir them around. Sprinkle with the parsley and serve.

variation
Substitute wholegrain mustard for the Dijon.

roast lamb with beans
agneau aux flageolets

The pre-salé lambs that graze on the salt marshes of Normandy, especially around Mont-St-Michel, are valued throughout France for their distinctively flavoured meat. A classic recipe is to braise a whole leg or shoulder with pale-green flageolet beans, but this is a quicker version using a rolled boneless leg.

SERVES 4–6

225 g/8 oz dried flageolet beans

1 large onion, quartered

6 large garlic cloves

1 bay leaf

sprigs of fresh rosemary

900 g/2 lb boneless leg of lamb, rolled and tied

2 tsp olive oil

40 g/1¹⁄₂ oz unsalted butter

2 tbsp chopped fresh flat-leaf parsley

150 ml/5 fl oz medium-dry cider, preferably
  from Normandy

about 150 ml/5 fl oz lamb stock or Vegetable Stock

salt and pepper

1 Put the beans in a large bowl, add enough water to cover by 2.5 cm/1 inch and leave to soak overnight.

2 The next day, drain and rinse the beans. Place the beans in a large saucepan and cover with twice their depth of water. Turn the heat to high, bring the water to the boil, skimming the surface as necessary, and boil for 10 minutes.

3 Drain the beans, then re-cover with more water and return to the boil. Add the onion, 4 of the garlic cloves and the bay leaf. Reduce the heat to low, cover the saucepan and leave to simmer for 60–90 minutes, or until the beans are tender. The exact cooking time will depend on how old the beans are; older beans will take longer to cook.

4 Meanwhile, heat the oven to 180°C/350°F/Gas Mark 4. Cut the remaining 2 cloves of garlic into thin slivers. Insert a couple of rosemary sprigs into the centre of the rolled lamb. Use the tip of a knife to make thin cuts all over the lamb, then insert the garlic slivers. Rub the lamb all over with the oil and season to taste with salt and pepper. Scatter over some rosemary leaves.

5 Place the lamb on a rack in a roasting tin and roast for 1 hour.

6 When the beans are tender, drain them well and discard the onion, garlic and bay leaf. Stir in the butter, parsley and salt and pepper to taste. Cover the beans with foil, shiny-side down, and keep warm.

7 When the lamb is cooked, transfer it to a serving platter, cover with foil and set aside to rest for 10 minutes. Meanwhile, remove the rack, tilt the roasting tin and use a large metal spoon to remove the fat from the surface of the pan juices.

8 Place the tin over a medium-high heat and deglaze it by stirring in the cider and scraping the sediment from the base of the pan. Bring to the boil and continue boiling until the juices reduce slightly, then add the stock and continue boiling until reduced by half. Season to taste with salt and pepper. Thinly slice the lamb and serve with the beans and pan juices.

spring lamb stew
navarin d'agneau printanier

A French culinary celebration of spring. This traditional recipe, which always includes baby turnips along with a varying selection of other new-season vegetables, gets a strong flavour boost from including bony pieces of best end of neck. These can be removed just before the stew goes to the table, but the meat next to the bones is tender and flavoursome. Almost uniquely among French stews, a navarin does not contain wine.

SERVES 4–6

500 g/1 lb 2 oz boneless shoulder of lamb, cut into
    5-cm/2-inch chunks

250 g/9 oz best end of neck lamb, chopped

2 tbsp caster sugar

140 g/5 oz unsalted butter

2 tbsp sunflower oil

2 tbsp plain flour

1 tbsp tomato purée

3 vine-ripened tomatoes, peeled, deseeded and chopped

3 garlic cloves, crushed

2 onions, chopped

600 ml/1 pint Chicken or Vegetable Stock

1 Bouquet Garni

200 g/7 oz baby turnips, peeled but left whole

200 g/7 oz baby carrots, scrubbed or peeled but left
    whole or chopped, depending on how young they are

200 g/7 oz pickling onions, peeled but left whole

200 g/7 oz small new potatoes, peeled but left whole

100 g/3¹/₂ oz shelled peas

salt and pepper

1 Preheat the oven to 190°C/375°F/Gas Mark 5. Season the lamb with 1 tablespoon of the sugar and salt and pepper to taste.

2 Melt 85 g/3 oz of the butter with the oil in a large flameproof casserole over a medium-high heat. Add the pieces of lamb shoulder and sauté until brown on all sides, working in batches as necessary. Remove the meat from the casserole as it browns and set aside. Add the pieces of lamb neck to the casserole and brown, then add them to the shoulder meat.

3 Pour off all but 2 tablespoons of the fat in the casserole. Return the meat to the casserole, sprinkle with the flour and sauté over a medium heat for 5 minutes, or until the flour browns.

4 Add the tomato purée, tomatoes, garlic, chopped onions and stock and bring to the boil, skimming the surface if necessary. Add the Bouquet Garni and season to taste with salt and pepper. Cover the casserole and transfer it to the oven to cook for 45 minutes.

5 Meanwhile, put the turnips, carrots and pickling onions in a large sauté or frying pan over a medium-high heat. Add the remaining butter and sugar, salt and pepper to taste and just enough water to cover the vegetables. Bring to the boil, then reduce the heat and simmer until the liquid evaporates and the vegetables are covered with a glaze, shaking the pan frequently.

6 After the stew has cooked for 45 minutes, add the glazed vegetables and the potatoes, re-cover the casserole and cook for a further 35 minutes. Add the peas and continue cooking for a further 10 minutes until the meat and all the vegetables are tender.

7 Use a large metal spoon to remove any excess fat from the surface. If the juices seem too thin, remove the meat and vegetables and keep warm while you boil the juices to reduce, then return the meat and vegetables to the casserole. Adjust the seasoning if necessary. Discard the Bouquet Garni before serving.

122 alsace sauerkraut with pork and sausages
choucroute garnie

No other dish illustrates the hearty cuisine of Alsace better than this huge feast of sauerkraut and smoked and fresh pork, which always takes centre stage at brasseries alsaciennes. There isn't any point in making this for a small number, and tradition dictates that the more diners there are, the greater the variety of meats that should be included. Boiled new potatoes are the traditional accompaniment.

SERVES 8–10

1 large ham knuckle, weighing 900 g/2 lb

450 g/1 lb smoked gammon steak, cut into large pieces

40 g/1¹/₂ oz goose fat or butter

1 tbsp sunflower oil (if using butter)

250 g/9 oz smoked or unsmoked lardons, to taste

3 garlic cloves, crushed

2 large onions, sliced

1 large carrot, peeled and diced

800 g/1 lb 12 oz bottled or canned sauerkraut, rinsed
   and drained

6 juniper berries

2 cloves

2 bay leaves

125 ml/4 fl oz Chicken Stock

225 ml/8 fl oz Alsace wine, such as Riesling or Sylvaner

450 g/1 lb small new potatoes

8–10 knockwurst sausages

8–10 frankfurters

4 or 5 boudin blanc sausages

4 or 5 boudin noir sausages

salt

Previous page Cattle rearing is still one of the most important rural industries in France today

1 Preheat the oven to 160°C/325°F/Gas Mark 3. Bring a large saucepan of water to the boil and add the ham knuckle. Reduce the heat to medium-low and leave to simmer for 35 minutes, skimming the surface as necessary. Add the smoked gammon pieces and continue simmering for a further 10 minutes. Drain the pieces of meat and set aside.

2 Meanwhile, melt the goose fat (or the butter and the oil, if using) in a large flameproof casserole over a medium-high heat. Add the lardons and fry for 2 minutes, or until they start to give off their fat. Use a slotted spoon to remove the lardons from the casserole and set aside.

3 Stir the garlic, onions and carrot into the fat in the casserole and sauté, stirring frequently, for 3–5 minutes until the onion is soft, but not brown. Use a large metal spoon to remove as much fat as possible from the casserole.

4 Return the lardons to the casserole. Add the sauerkraut and stir in the juniper berries, cloves and bay leaves. Pour in the stock and wine and bring to the boil, stirring, then cover the casserole tightly and put it in the oven for 25 minutes.

5 Meanwhile, bring a large saucepan of salted water to the boil and heat another large saucepan of unsalted water until it simmers. Add the potatoes to the salted water and return to the boil, leaving them to boil for 20 minutes, or until they are tender. Drain the potatoes. When they are cool enough to handle, peel them and set aside.

6 Add the knockwurst, frankfurter, boudin blanc and boudin noir sausages to the simmering water and simmer for 15 minutes, or until cooked through. Drain them well.*

7 Remove the casserole from the oven and arrange the ham knuckle, gammon pieces, sausages and potatoes on the sauerkraut. Re-cover and return it to the oven for 15 minutes for the flavours to blend.

8 Spoon the sauerkraut onto a warmed serving platter. Top with the sausages and gammon steak and arrange the potatoes around the edge. Remove the meat from the knuckle in large chunks and place on top.

*cook's tip
Take care not to let the water boil in Step 6 or the sausages might burst.

pork chops with calvados and apples
côtes de porc à la normande

124

Apples are synonymous with Normandy, so most recipes labelled as à la normande *are certain to contain them in one form or another. This rich but simple dish, with glazed apples as the garnish, is also flavoured with Calvados, an apple brandy, and cider.*

MAKES 4

90 g/3¹/₄ oz butter

2 apples, such as Granny Smith, peeled, cored and each cut into 8 wedges

1 tbsp caster sugar

1 tbsp sunflower oil

4 pork loin chops, about 2 cm/³/₄ inch thick

2 shallots, chopped

¹/₂ tbsp fresh thyme leaves or 1 tsp dried thyme

6 tbsp Calvados

125 ml/4 fl oz sweet or dry cider, to taste, ideally from Normandy

250 ml/9 fl oz double cream

salt and pepper

1 Preheat the oven to its lowest temperature. Melt 30 g/1 oz of the butter in a sauté or frying pan, large enough to hold the pork chops in a single layer, over a medium heat. Add the apple wedges, sprinkle with the sugar and sauté for 5–6 minutes, turning them several times, until golden brown. Transfer to an ovenproof dish and keep warm in the oven. Wipe out the pan.

2 Melt another 30 g/1 oz of the butter with the oil in the pan over a medium-high heat. Using a pair of tongs, fry the pork chops one-by-one, fat-edge down, until the fat is golden.

3 Lay all the chops flat in the pan and cook for 5 minutes. Turn the chops over and continue cooking for a further 5–6 minutes until cooked through and tender. Transfer the chops to an ovenproof serving dish, cover with foil, shiny-side down, and keep warm in the oven. Pour off the excess fat and wipe the pan with kitchen paper.

4 Melt the remaining butter in the pan. Add the shallots and thyme and sauté for 2–3 minutes, or until the shallots are soft, but not brown. Add the Calvados and bring to the boil, scraping the sediment from the base of the pan. Stir in the cider and cream and return to the boil, stirring. Continue boiling until reduced by half.

5 Tip any juices from the chops into the sauce and return the sauce to the boil. Season to taste with salt and pepper. Spoon the sauce over the chops and garnish with the apple wedges.

French cities boast a rich cultural heritage in the form of palaces, museums, monuments and art collections

The pairing of pork and prunes is a fantastic flavour combination that appears on restaurant menus all along the Loire Valley, with the sweetness of the fruit complementing the rich meat. This recipe is from near Tours, which got its name from its many ancient towers, or tours, *some of which once stored prunes for winter use.*

pork with prunes 127
porc aux pruneaux

SERVES 4

16 ready-to-eat prunes

4 tbsp brandy or Madeira

2 tbsp water

600 g/1 lb 5 oz pork fillet

30 g/1 oz unsalted butter

1 tbsp sunflower oil

125 ml/4 fl oz double cream or crème fraîche

squeeze of lemon juice

salt and pepper

1 Put the prunes in a saucepan with 2 tablespoons of the brandy and the water and simmer over a low heat, uncovered, for 10 minutes, or until the prunes are very tender, but still holding their shape. Strain off any excess liquid and set the prunes aside.

2 Cut the pork fillet into 2-cm/³⁄₄-inch slices and season to taste with salt and pepper. Melt the butter with the oil in a large sauté or frying pan over a medium-high heat. Add the pork slices and fry for 2–3 minutes on each side until cooked through, working in batches if necessary.

3 Return all the pork slices to the pan and remove the pan from the heat. Warm the remaining brandy in a ladle or small saucepan, ignite and pour it over the pork slices to flambé.

4 When the flames die down, stir in the cream and bring to the boil, stirring constantly, until reduced.

5 Add the prunes to the pan and warm through. Season to taste with salt and pepper and a little lemon juice.

Ancient and beautiful architecture, testament to a rich past, is evident in the Loire Valley and all over France

A real stick-to-the-ribs winter warmer, this traditional Gascony bean feast, with its crunchy breadcrumb topping, has so many variations that it is virtually impossible to give a definitive recipe. What is important, however, is to use small, white haricot beans that hold their shape during the long cooking.

SERVES 6–8

300 g/10½ oz dried white haricot beans, soaked for
  at least 5 hours or according to packet instructions
140 g/5 oz plain or smoked belly of pork, rind removed,
  cut into thick pieces
4 large garlic cloves, chopped
1 large bouquet garni of 4 sprigs of fresh parsley,
  6 sprigs of fresh thyme and 1 bay leaf, tied together
large pinch of quatre épices
8 Toulouse sausages
4 pieces of goose or duck confit, about 400 g/14 oz
400 g/14 oz boneless shoulder of pork, cut into
  5-cm/2-inch chunks
Chicken or Vegetable Stock, if needed
200 g/7 oz day-old French bread, made into fine
  breadcrumbs
8 tbsp finely chopped fresh flat-leaf parsley
salt and pepper

1 Rinse the beans, then put them in a large heavy-based saucepan with water to cover over a high heat. Bring to the boil and boil rapidly for 10 minutes, then drain. Return the beans to the wiped pan with 5 cm/2 inches of water to cover and bring to the boil. Reduce the heat to a simmer and skim the surface until the grey foam stops rising.

2 Add the belly of pork, garlic, bouquet garni, quatre épices and pepper, to taste. Adjust the heat so that bubbles just appear around the edge, then partially cover the pan and leave the beans to simmer for 1-1½ hours, or according to the packet instructions, until the

beans are just slightly less than tender. The older the beans are, the longer they will take to cook. Do not let them boil or the skins will split.

3 Meanwhile, preheat the grill to high. Grill the sausages, turning them frequently, just until the casings are browned, then set aside.

4 Heat about 2 tablespoons of fat from the confit in a frying pan over a medium-high heat. Add the pork chunks and fry until brown on each side, then set aside.

5 Preheat the oven to 150°C/300°F/Gas Mark 2. When the beans are almost tender, place a large sieve over a large bowl and strain the beans, discarding the bouquet garni, but reserving the cooking liquid.

6 Put half the beans in a large flameproof casserole. Add the sausages, goose or duck confit and pork chunks. Season to taste with salt and pepper, then cover with the remaining beans.

7 Pour in enough of the reserved cooking liquid to cover all the ingredients, topping up with the stock if necessary. Mix the breadcrumbs and parsley together, then spread half thickly over the surface.

8 Put in the oven and bake, uncovered, for 4 hours. After 1 hour, use the back of a spoon to lightly push the breadcrumbs into the liquid, repeating this twice more at hourly intervals.

9 After 3 hours, sprinkle the top with the remaining breadcrumbs and do not press into the liquid. Return the casserole to the oven and continue baking for an hour, or until the top is golden and crisp. If the liquid appears to evaporate too quickly, pour in a little extra stock at the edges. Serve from the casserole.

130
puy lentils with sausages
saucisses aux lentilles du puy

The tiny, round, green-grey lentils from the region of Le Puy, in the mountainous Auvergne, are often labelled as 'poor man's caviar', as a tribute to their outstanding flavour at an affordable price. Protected by their own appellation contrôlée, *Puy lentils are also favoured by cooks for their ability to hold their shape during cooking. This simple supper dish is like a warm lentil salad. The sharpness of the vinegar cuts through the rich, earthy flavour of the lentils.*

SERVES 4–6

2 tbsp sunflower oil

1 large onion, finely chopped

2 large garlic cloves, finely chopped

2 carrots, peeled and cut into 5-mm/¼-inch dice

400 g/14 oz Puy lentils, rinsed

½ tsp dried thyme

1 bay leaf

4–12 fresh sausages, such as Toulouse*

5 tbsp Vinaigrette or Garlic Vinaigrette

2 tbsp chopped fresh flat-leaf parsley

salt and pepper

1 Heat the oil in a heavy-based saucepan with a tight-fitting lid over a medium-high heat. Add the onion, garlic and carrots and stir around for 5 minutes, or until the onion is soft, but not brown.

2 Stir in the lentils. Add enough water to cover the lentils by 2.5 cm/1 inch and bring to the boil, skimming the surface if necessary. Stir in the thyme and bay leaf, then reduce the heat to low, cover the pan tightly and leave to simmer for 10 minutes.

3 Uncover the saucepan and continue simmering for 15–20 minutes, or until the carrots and lentils are tender. If the water is absorbed before the lentils are tender, add a little more and continue cooking.

4 Meanwhile, preheat the grill to high. Brush the grill rack with oil, lightly prick the sausages all over and grill, turning them occasionally, until they are cooked through and the skins are crispy brown. Set aside and keep warm.

5 The lentils should absorb all the water by the time they are tender, but if any remains on the surface, drain it off. Transfer the lentils to a large serving bowl. Add the Vinaigrette to the hot lentils and stir around so that they are well coated.

6 Add salt and pepper to taste, then stir in the parsley. Serve the hot lentils with the sausages.

cook's tip

French *charcuteries* sell a seemingly limitless variety of sausages. Some are air-dried and ready to eat (*saucissons*), but fresh sausages that require grilling or boiling (*saucisses*) are the ones to buy for this dish. Mild-flavoured, country-style Toulouse sausage (*saucisse de Toulouse*) is only one example. Others to try include *saucisse de Morteau*, a smoked pork preparation from Franche-Comté, or *saucisse de merguez*, a small, spicy beef sausage originally from North Africa. Supermarkets and Muslim butchers often sell these and you need to allow 4 or 5 per person as they are so small.

veal chops with wild mushroom sauce

côtes de veau sauce à la forestière

In autumn French markets offer a fantastic display of wild mushrooms – all quickly bought by the country's numerous connoisseurs. Gathering wild mushrooms is such a popular pastime that French pharmacies offer an identification service to help avoid fatal accidents.

MAKES 4

4 veal loin chops, 2 cm/³/₄ inch thick

garlic– or paprika-flavoured olive oil

salt and pepper

for the Wild Mushroom Sauce

300 ml/10 fl oz Madeira

55 g/2 oz butter

2 shallots, finely chopped

500 g/1 lb 2 oz mixed wild mushrooms, such as ceps, chanterelles, morels and shiitakes, wiped, trimmed and sliced if large

500 ml/18 fl oz Vegetable Stock

freshly grated nutmeg

salt and pepper

1 To make the Wild Mushroom Sauce, put the Madeira in a small saucepan over a high heat and boil until it reduces by half, then set aside. Melt the butter in a large sauté or frying pan over a medium-high heat. Add the shallots and sauté for 2–3 minutes, or until soft, but not brown.

2 Stir the mushrooms into the pan and continue sautéeing until they give off their liquid. Pour in the stock and bring to the boil, stirring. Reduce the heat to low and leave the stock to simmer until it reduces by half. Stir in the reduced Madeira and continue simmering until only about 6 tablespoons of the liquid are left. Add a few gratings of nutmeg, then season to taste with salt and pepper.

3 Meanwhile, preheat the grill to high. Lightly brush the veal chops with the oil and season to taste with salt and pepper. Transfer to the grill rack. Grill the veal chops for 3 minutes. Turn them over, brush again with the oil and season to taste with salt and pepper. Continue grilling for a further 3–4 minutes until tender and cooked as desired. Transfer the chops to serving plates and spoon the Wild Mushroom Sauce alongside.

variations

When fresh wild mushrooms are out of season, soak 55 g/2 oz dried ceps or porcini in hot water for 20 minutes, then drain.

Italian gourmet food shops sell porcini-flavoured olive oil, which is also excellent to use in this dish.

Enjoying a leisurely beer, wine or coffee at a French café is a simple pleasure not to be missed

134 veal with mushrooms in a cream sauce
blanquette de veau

This creamy stew never loses its popularity and is an example of cuisine bourgeoise *at its most traditional. It is also one of the few French dishes that is regularly served with plain, boiled long-grain rice. Young chefs, however, often now prepare a simple risotto as an accompaniment.*

SERVES 4–6

900 g/2 lb topside of veal, cut into 5-cm/2-inch cubes

2 veal bones, chopped

450 ml/16 fl oz dry white wine, such as Chinon

1 leek, halved, rinsed and sliced

1 large onion, studded with 5 cloves

1 large carrot, peeled and sliced

1 star anise

1 Bouquet Garni

85 g/3 oz butter

1 tbsp sunflower oil

225 g/8 oz button mushrooms, sliced

2 tbsp plain flour

freshly grated nutmeg

1 tbsp lemon juice

2 large egg yolks

150 ml/5 fl oz crème fraîche

salt and pepper

1 Place the veal and bones in a large flameproof casserole over a medium-high heat with the wine and enough water to cover by 4 cm/1½ inches. Slowly bring to the boil, skimming the surface as necessary.

2 When the grey foam stops rising, add the leek, onion, carrot, star anise, Bouquet Garni and salt to taste. Reduce the heat to low, cover the casserole tightly and leave the meat to simmer for 45 minutes, or until it is tender.

3 Meanwhile, preheat the oven to its lowest temperature. Melt 30 g/1 oz of the butter with the oil in a small sauté or frying pan over a medium-high heat. When the butter stops foaming, add the mushrooms and sauté for 5–7 minutes until they are browned. They will absorb the fat at first, then give it off again. Set the mushrooms aside and keep warm in the oven.

4 When the meat is tender, use a slotted spoon to transfer it to a serving platter. Spoon a little of the cooking liquid over the meat, cover with foil, shiny-side down, and transfer to the oven to keep warm.

5 Strain and reserve the cooking liquid, discarding the flavouring vegetables and Bouquet Garni. Put the cooking liquid in a saucepan and simmer over a low heat.

6 Melt the remaining butter in the wiped casserole over a medium heat. Stir in the flour and continue stirring for 2 minutes to cook out the 'raw' flavour and make a thick, smooth paste.

7 Remove the pan from the heat and slowly whisk in 300 ml/10 fl oz of the reserved cooking liquid, whisking constantly, to make a smooth sauce. Season to taste with nutmeg and salt and pepper. Return the pan to a low heat and leave the sauce to simmer.

8 Beat the lemon juice, egg yolks and crème fraîche together in a large bowl. Slowly pour the sauce into this mixture, whisking constantly. Stir in the mushrooms and any juices that have accumulated on the plate with the meat, then taste, and adjust the seasoning if necessary. Spoon the sauce over the meat and serve.*

*cook's tip

Reheat any leftovers using a *bain-marie* to avoid curdling the eggs in the sauce.

136

stuffed veal olives
paupiettes de veau

From the area around Le Mans, where veal is one of the local specialities, this recipe makes an ideal main course for a French-style dinner party, as all the cooking can be done in advance and the dish reheated at the last minute.

SERVES 4

8 veal escalopes, about 100 g/3½ oz each

175 g/6 oz unsalted butter

2 tbsp sunflower oil

6 spring onions, very finely chopped

300 g/10½ oz ham, any excess fat removed, finely chopped

finely grated rind and juice of 1 orange

85 g/3 oz fine fresh white breadcrumbs

2 tbsp chopped fresh flat-leaf parsley, plus extra to garnish

1 tbsp snipped fresh chives

2 eggs, beaten

300 ml/10 fl oz dry white wine

300 ml/10 fl oz veal or Chicken Stock or water

salt and pepper

sprigs of fresh flat-leaf parsley, to garnish

for the beurre manié

15 g/½ oz unsalted butter, softened

15 g/½ oz plain flour

1 Working with 1 veal escalope at a time, place it between 2 sheets of greaseproof paper and use a rolling pin to bash it until it is evenly thin. Continue until all the escalopes are pounded, then set aside.

2 Melt 85 g/3 oz of the butter with 1 tablespoon of the oil in a large sauté or frying pan with a tight-fitting lid over a medium heat. Add the spring onions and sauté for 2–3 minutes until soft, but not coloured.

3 Meanwhile, combine the ham, half the orange rind and juice, the breadcrumbs, herbs and salt and pepper to taste in a bowl. Stir in the spring onions, then add the eggs and beat together.

4 Again, working with 1 veal escalope at a time, spread one-eighth of the stuffing over each escalope, then roll up like a Swiss roll. Use kitchen string to tie up each veal olive securely.

5 Melt the remaining butter with the remaining oil in the washed and dried sauté or frying pan over a medium heat. Add the veal olives and sauté to brown all over. Pour in the wine and stock with the remaining orange rind and juice and salt and pepper to taste.

6 Slowly bring the liquid to the boil, then reduce the heat to low, cover the pan and simmer for 25 minutes, or until the veal is tender when pierced with the tip of a knife. Transfer the veal olives to a serving platter, cover with foil, shiny-side down, and set aside.*

7 Meanwhile, to make the *beurre manié*, mash the butter and flour together to make a thick paste.

8 Bring the cooking liquid to the boil, then add small amounts of the *beurre manié*, whisking constantly and only adding more when the previous amount has been incorporated, until the sauce is thick and shiny. Taste and adjust the seasoning if necessary. Slice the veal olives widthways, spoon over the sauce and serve, garnished with parsley sprigs.

cook's tip

If any breadcrumbs escape from the veal rolls while they are simmering in Step 6, strain the liquid before adding the *beurre manié*.

FISH &
SHELLFISH

140 With long coastlines along the English Channel, the Atlantic Ocean and the Mediterranean Sea, not to mention many inland waterways, French cooks and diners have a huge variety of fresh fish and shellfish to choose from. Coastal areas are naturally renowned for their seafood preparations, but fish and shellfish are enjoyed throughout the country and French fishmongers (*poissonniers*) can be relied upon to offer a good selection whatever the season. An excellent transportation system means that French cooks are spoilt for choice from fresh-from-the-water displays on market stalls and supermarket counters as well as at fishmongers.

Boulogne-sur-Mer draws British day-trippers in search of freshly caught seafood and its weekly food market. The quaint seafood restaurants along the sleepy harbourside disguise the fact that this is France's largest commercial port and one of the busiest in Europe. Turbot (*turbout*) and sole (*sole*), the kings of the flatfish family, are part of the regular catch. Their delicate flesh is best simply cooked and the recipe for Sole Meunière (see page 167) is a classic preparation that is equally suitable for the sole's less prized cousins. Skate (*raie*), another delicacy caught off northern France, is bought for the gelatinous, sweet flesh on its wide wings.

The cool waters along northern and western France also yield cod (*cabillaud*), ling (*lingue*), mackerel (*maquereau*) and monkfish (*lotte*), as well as tonnes of herring, most of which are destined to be smoked. A large part of Brittany's sardine catch supplies commercial canneries, while sea urchins (*oursin*), somewhat of an acquired taste, are a speciality of Brittany's seafood restaurants.

Inland, popular freshwater fish, such as trout (*truite*), pike (*brochet*) and perch (*perche*), along with eels (*anguilles*) and carp (*carpe*), find their way into numerous stews called *matelotes*. Trout with Mussels and Prawns (see page 156) is a speciality of Dieppe on Normandy's coast.

Anyone who has ever enjoyed a glorious seafood platter (*plateau de fruits de mer*), piled high with raw and cooked shellfish (*coquillage*), might have the fishermen from France's west coast to thank. Some of the best molluscs and crustaceans in Europe are caught here, including sweet lobsters, one of the gems of Brittany. Not many years ago, oysters (*huîtres*) were only served in months that contained an 'R' in their names, but today large oyster beds mean that they are available all year round. *Belons*, flat oysters from off the Brittany coast, and *Gravette d'Arcachon*, from near La Rochelle in Bordeaux, are considered the best. Other shellfish delicacies include clams (*clovisses* or *palourdes*), cockles (*coques*) and whelks (*bulots*). Large bowls of steamed mussels in white wine with garlic and parsley (*moules à la marinière*) are served

Stormclouds gather over the rooftops here, but the mild climate of France is a boon to its food and wine industries

Left France's famous Mediterranean coast caters for mass tourism as well as being home to rich fishing grounds

Right French coastal towns and cities offer a huge variety of freshly prepared gastronomic delights

in restaurants all over France, but in Normandy cream and cider are used for a local flavour in Mussels in Cider (see page 144). The cultivated mussels from the Atlantic (*bouchet*) are smaller than those from the warmer waters further south.

It is along the Med, however, that one really appreciates the bounty of France's seafood. Marseille's daily fish market, for example, serves up a dazzling display of seafood: anchovy (*anchois*), gilthead bream (*daurade*), grey mullet (*mulet*), gurnard (*grondin*), octopus (*poulpe*), rascasse (*rascasse*), red mullet (*rouget*) and squid (*encornet*) are among the local species. Southern French seafood cookery is summed up in the local expression that fish 'should live in water, but die in olive oil'. Bouillabaisse, an elaborate fish soup, is the crown jewel of Provençale cuisine, but other regional specialities include Grilled Red Mullet with Fennel and Peppers (see page 169) and Tuna with Green Sauce (see page 168). The Basques, in the southwest, also have a long history as fishermen, and Basque-style Cod (see page 154) captures local flavours with red and green peppers and garlic.

Most of the fish (*poissons*) and shellfish available in France are familiar in other countries, but some specimens are difficult to buy outside France. Two specific examples are *sander*, a freshwater pike-perch from the Loire Valley, appreciated for its delicate flesh and classically served with a butter sauce, and *rascasse*. For many bouillabaisse connoisseurs, the dish isn't authentic if it doesn't contain this spiky fish with its sweet flesh.

Simplicity is the key to successful seafood cookery. Anyone new to seafood cooking should try the French

technique of wrapping fish fillets and other ingredients in foil parcels or cooking *en papillote* to preserve the tenderness. Salmon with Leeks in Foil (see page 147) and Monkfish with Courgettes and Mushrooms in Foil (see page 158) are two examples that are virtually foolproof. Freshness is the all-important consideration when buying seafood. Do not accept any fish that doesn't have bright eyes and healthy looking, red-pink gills. If you press your finger into the flesh, it shouldn't leave an impression. Transfer the fish to a refrigerator as soon as possible and cook it on the day of purchase.

144

mussels in cider
moules à la crème normande

Fish stalls in the coastal ports of Normandy offer an abundance of freshly caught shiny black mussels. Mussels steamed with white wine, garlic and parsley (moules à la marinière) are standard restaurant and bistro fare throughout France, but in Normandy the dish is given a regional flavour with the local cider and cream.

SERVES 4–6

2 kg/4 lb 8 oz live mussels*

4 tbsp sunflower oil

2 onions, finely chopped

1 large garlic clove, finely chopped

400 ml/14 fl oz dry cider, ideally from Normandy

1 bay leaf

200 ml/7 fl oz double cream

salt and pepper

chopped fresh flat-leaf parsley, to garnish

slices French bread, to serve

1 To prepare the mussels, cut off and discard any beards, then scrub any dirty shells. Discard any mussels with broken shells or open ones that do not instantly close when tapped.

2 Heat the oil in a large heavy-based saucepan with a tight-fitting lid over a medium-high heat. Add the onions and sauté for 3 minutes, then add the garlic and continue sautéeing for a further 2 minutes, or until the onions are soft, but not coloured.

3 Add the cider and bay leaf and bring the cider to the boil. Continue boiling until the cider is reduced by half to concentrate the flavour, then reduce the heat to very low.

4 Add the mussels to the saucepan. Reduce the heat to very low, cover the pan tightly and simmer for 4 minutes, shaking the pan frequently.

5 When the mussels are all open, transfer them to a large bowl, cover and keep warm. Discard any mussels that do not open.

6 Line a large sieve with a piece of muslin or kitchen cloth and place over a large bowl. Strain the cooking juices into the bowl, then return them to the washed pan. Add the cream and bring the cooking juices to the boil and boil until reduced by one-third.

7 Season the cooking juices to taste with salt and pepper, then pour over the mussels and sprinkle with parsley. Serve with plenty of French bread to mop up the delicious juices.

*cook's tip
Farmed mussels tend to be much cleaner than those harvested in the wild, so it might not be necessary to strain the cooking juices through muslin in Step 6 to remove the small amount of grit.

Freshwater fish such as pike, perch, eel and carp can be found on the menus of many French restaurants

146 # crisp salmon with sorrel sauce
saumon avec sauce oseille

For many French chefs there is only one way to cook salmon, and that is à l'unilateral, *or on one side only. This technique produces a rosy-pink 'rare' flesh that showcases the taste of really fresh salmon.*

SERVES 4

4 centre-cut salmon fillets with the skin on, about
   150 g/5¹/₂ oz each and 2.5 cm/1 inch thick
¹/₂ tbsp sunflower oil, plus extra for brushing the skins
40 g/1¹/₂ oz unsalted butter
sea salt and pepper

for the Sorrel Sauce

250 g/9 oz fresh sorrel leaves, thick stems removed,
   well rinsed
30 g/1 oz unsalted butter
2 tbsp double cream
1 tsp finely grated lemon rind
pinch of cayenne pepper (optional)
salt and pepper

1 Cut 3 or 4 thin scores through each salmon skin, without cutting into the flesh. Lightly brush the salmon skins with a little oil and sprinkle with salt and pepper to taste.

2 Melt the butter with the oil in a heavy-based sauté or frying pan, large enough to hold the salmon steaks in a single layer, over a high heat. Add the salmon fillets, skin-side down, and cook for 7 minutes, or until the skin is crisp and browned, shaking the pan occasionally so the fillets don't stick.*

3 Meanwhile, to make the Sorrel Sauce, put the sorrel leaves and butter in a heavy-based saucepan over a medium heat. Stir until the leaves wilt, then stir in the cream and lemon rind. When the cream is hot, add salt and pepper to taste and a pinch of cayenne, if you like. Serve the salmon with the sauce on the side.

*cook's tip
If the salmon is too rare after cooking in Step 2 for your taste, cover the pan tightly and leave it to cook for a further 2 minutes.

salmon with leeks in foil

saumon aux poireaux en papillote

For a stylish French meal, this easy recipe is difficult to beat. It comes from the dynamic Parisian Paule Caillat. She runs Promenades Gourmandes, giving French cooking lessons in Paris, as well as taking students behind the scenes in restaurants, bakeries and food shops. Cooking fish en papillote is a French technique that makes it almost impossible to overcook fish, and for dinner parties the foil parcels can be prepared earlier in the day, ready to put in the oven when you sit down for the first course.

SERVES 4

2 tbsp olive oil, plus extra for the foil parcels

4 large leeks, white part only, halved, rinsed and
   finely sliced

12 lemon slices

4 salmon fillets, all skin and bones removed, about
   140 g/5 oz each

6 tbsp finely chopped fresh flat-leaf parsley or a mixture
   of chives, mint, parsley and tarragon

4 tbsp crème fraîche

salt and pepper

1 Heat the oil in a heavy-based saucepan with a tight-fitting lid over a medium-low heat. Stir in the leeks and reduce the heat to low. Cover the saucepan and simmer for 8–10 minutes until the leeks are tender, but not coloured. Season to taste with salt and pepper.

2 Meanwhile, preheat the oven to 220°C/425°F/Gas Mark 7. Cut 4 squares of foil large enough to loosely fold over each piece of salmon. Brush the centre of each piece of foil with a little olive oil. Arrange 3 lemon slices over the oil, then top with a salmon fillet.

3 Spread the leeks equally over the salmon fillets, then top with the herbs and 1 tablespoon of crème fraîche each. Fold the foil over each fillet and fold the edges in twice so that none of the juices can escape during cooking.*

4 Place the foil parcels on a baking tray and transfer to the oven to bake for 12 minutes, or until the flesh flakes easily when you open a parcel to test.

5 To serve, transfer the salmon and leeks to warmed plates and spoon over the juices that will have accumulated in the foil parcels.

*cook's tip

Do not wrap the foil too tightly around the salmon and leeks in Step 3. It is important to leave space for steam to develop so that the fish stays moist. Baking paper can also be used to wrap the salmon and leeks. The paper will brown and puff during cooking. Transfer the parcel to warmed plates and let each diner open their own to appreciate the wonderful aromas.

seafood in a light broth with vegetables

poisson à la nage

A la nage *translates as 'swimming', and tender pieces of poached seafood are literally swimming in a pool of saffron-scented broth in this stylish dish.*

SERVES 4

small pinch of saffron threads

55 g/2 oz unsalted butter

2 carrots, peeled and cut into julienne strips

2 celery sticks, cut into julienne strips

1 courgette, cut into julienne strips

1 shallot, very finely chopped

2 garlic cloves, very finely chopped

1 Bouquet Garni

200 ml/7 fl oz dry white wine

200 ml/7 fl oz water

8 pieces of mixed fresh fish, such as salmon fillets and
   monkfish medallions, or only 1 type of fish, all skin and
   bones removed, about 125 g/4¹/₂ oz each

250 ml/9 fl oz crème fraîche

salt and pepper

fresh chervil sprigs, to garnish

1 Put the saffron threads in a small dry frying pan over a high heat and toast, stirring constantly, for 1 minute, or until you can smell the aroma. Immediately tip the saffron threads out of the pan and set aside.

2 Melt the butter in a sauté or frying pan with a tight-fitting lid, large enough to hold the fish in a single layer, over a medium heat. Add the carrots, celery, courgette, shallot, garlic, Bouquet Garni and salt and pepper to taste and sauté for 3 minutes, without letting the vegetables colour.*

3 Meanwhile, put the wine and water in a saucepan over a high heat and bring to the boil, then boil for 2 minutes. Pour the boiling liquid over the vegetables, reduce the heat to low and simmer for 5 minutes. Remove from the heat and discard the Bouquet Garni.

4 Place the fish over the vegetables, cover the pan and simmer for 5 minutes, or until the fish is cooked through and flakes easily. The exact time will depend on the thickness and selection of fish, so start testing after 3 minutes to avoid overcooking.

5 Transfer the fish and vegetables to a warmed bowl and spoon over a little of the poaching liquid. Cover with foil, shiny-side down, and set aside.

6 Stir the crème fraîche and saffron threads into the cooking liquid and bring to the boil, stirring. Continue boiling for 3–5 minutes until the poaching liquid is reduced. Taste and adjust the seasoning.

7 Place a mound of vegetables in the centre of 4 soup plates and top with the fish. Spoon the reduced cooking liquid over and garnish with the chervil.

*cook's tip

The carrots and celery sticks can be cut into very fine dice rather than julienne strips, or cut into very thin strips using a vegetable peeler. They can be prepared several hours in advance and stored in a bowl of cold water in the refrigerator. Just remember to dry them thoroughly before adding them to the butter in Step 2.

150 poached trout with butter sauce
truite pochée au beurre blanc

White butter sauce, or beurre blanc, *may have originated in Brittany, where it is made with crisp-tasting Muscadet, the wine grown around Nantes at the western edge of the Loire. The richness of the sauce makes it a perfect foil for any fish simply poached in* court bouillon, *a flavoured liquid.*

SERVES 4

4 rainbow trout, fins removed and gutted, with head
    left on or removed, rinsed inside and out and dried

to garnish
8 lemon slices
8 sprigs of fresh tarragon

for the Court Bouillon
2 litres/3$\frac{1}{2}$ pints water
500 ml/18 fl oz white wine, such as Muscadet
3 carrots, peeled and chopped
3 leeks, halved, rinsed and chopped
3 celery sticks, chopped
2 onions, sliced
1 Bouquet Garni
1 bay leaf
2 tbsp sea salt
5 black peppercorns, lightly crushed

for the Butter Sauce
3 tbsp very finely chopped shallots
2 bay leaves
6 black peppercorns, lightly crushed
3 tbsp white wine, such as Muscadet
3 tbsp white wine vinegar
1$\frac{1}{2}$ tbsp double cream
175 g/6 oz unsalted butter, cut into small pieces
2 tsp chopped fresh tarragon
salt and pepper

1 Up to a day in advance, make the Court Bouillon. Place the water, wine, vegetables, Bouquet Garni, bay leaf, sea salt and peppercorns in a large saucepan over a high heat and bring to the boil. Reduce the heat until bubbles just break the surface and leave to slow boil for 30 minutes, uncovered.

2 Strain the Court Bouillon into a bowl and discard the flavourings. Set aside and leave to cool. The Court Bouillon is now ready to use, or it can be covered and refrigerated for up to 1 day.

3 When you are ready to cook, make the Butter Sauce. Put the shallots, bay leaves, peppercorns, wine and vinegar in a small saucepan over a medium-high heat and boil until reduced to about 1 tablespoon. Strain the mixture through a non-metallic sieve, then return the liquid to the saucepan.

4 Stir the cream into the liquid and bring to the boil, then reduce the heat to low. Whisk in the butter, piece by piece, not adding the next until the previous one is melted. Whisking constantly and lifting the pan off the heat occasionally will help prevent the sauce from separating. Stir in the tarragon and salt and pepper

to taste.* Cover and keep warm while the fish poaches. This sauce cannot be reheated or it will separate.

5 Meanwhile, put the fish in a sauté or frying pan large enough to hold them side by side. Pour over enough Court Bouillon to cover and slowly bring to the boil. Immediately reduce the heat to very low and leave the fish to simmer for 8–10 minutes until the flesh flakes easily.

6 Remove the fish from the liquid and pat dry. The fish can now be served whole or skinned and filleted. Serve on warmed plates with the sauce spooned over, garnished with lemon slices and tarragon.

*cook's tip
If the sauce tastes too acidic in Step 4, whisk in another piece of butter. If it's bland, add a little wine vinegar.

Nîmes, in Languedoc, is known for the preparation of this traditional dish, which, in the days before refrigerated transport, once took the place of fresh seafood in the winter. It was also the traditional Friday evening meal before the Catholic Church lifted the restriction on eating meat on Fridays. Although French supermarkets now provide a seemingly limitless supply of fresh seafood all year round, brandade de morue *remains popular, and for many French families the Christmas Eve feast wouldn't be complete without a large bowl of this creamy dish. Begin preparing it at least two days in advance to allow enough time to soak the salt cod.*

SERVES 4–6
700 g/1 lb 9 oz salt cod
300 ml/10 fl oz olive oil
2 large garlic cloves, very finely chopped
300 ml/10 fl oz single cream
lemon juice, to taste
pepper
Fried Croûtes, to serve

to garnish
black olives, stoned and halved
chopped fresh flat-leaf parsley

1 Cut or break the salt cod into pieces that will fit in a large bowl of water, then leave to soak for up to 48 hours, replacing the water with fresh water every 8 hours or so to remove the saltiness.

2 Drain the salt cod, then transfer it to a saucepan and cover with fresh water. Slowly bring to a simmer and leave the salt cod to simmer for 15–20 minutes until it is tender and flakes easily.

3 Meanwhile, heat the oil in a heavy-based saucepan just until the surface shimmers. Add the garlic and set aside to infuse.

creamed salt cod
brandade de morue

153

4 Drain the salt cod. When it is cool enough to handle, remove all the skin and small bones. Then flake the flesh into a food processor.

5 Reheat the garlic-infused oil and heat the cream in a separate pan. With the food processor's motor running, add about 2 tablespoons of the oil, then 2 tablespoons of the cream to the cod. Continue adding the oil and cream until they are absorbed and the cod has a consistency of mashed potatoes.

6 Taste the mixture and add pepper and lemon juice to taste. Extra salt shouldn't be necessary. Mound the salt cod mixture on a serving platter and garnish with the olive halves, then sprinkle parsley over. Serve with the Fried Croûtes.*

*cook's tip
If the finished dish still tastes too salty, mash some floury potatoes and beat them into the mixture.

Much of France's coastline is ruggedly picturesque, and no area more so than Finistère in western Brittany

154 basque-style cod
cabillaud à la basquaise

*Red and green peppers, tomatoes and lots of garlic
are typically used to flavour the seafood in the
Basque region, where France meets Spain, and the
Spanish influence is evident in the local architecture
as well as the cuisine.*

SERVES 4

3 tbsp olive oil

4 cod fillets, about 175 g/6 oz each, all skin and bones
   removed and patted dry

1 tbsp plain flour

1 large onion, finely chopped

4 large tomatoes, peeled, deseeded and chopped

2 large garlic cloves, crushed

150 ml/5 fl oz dry white wine

1/2 tsp paprika, to taste

2 red peppers, chargrilled, peeled, deseeded and cut
   into strips

2 green peppers, chargrilled, peeled, deseeded and cut
   into strips

zest of 1 lemon, in broad strips

salt and pepper

finely chopped fresh flat-leaf parsley, to garnish

1 Preheat the oven to 200°C/400°F/Gas Mark 6. Heat
1 tablespoon of the oil in a flameproof casserole
over a medium-high heat. Very lightly dust 1 side of
each cod fillet with the flour, seasoned to taste with salt
and pepper. Fry, floured-side down, for 2 minutes, or
until just golden. Set aside.

2 Wipe out the casserole, then heat the remaining oil
over a medium-high heat. Add the onion and sauté
for 5 minutes, or until soft, but not browned.

3 Stir in the tomatoes, garlic, wine, paprika and salt
and pepper to taste and bring to the boil. Reduce
the heat and simmer for 5 minutes, stirring occasionally.

4 Stir the red and green peppers into the casserole
with the lemon strips and bring to the boil. Lay the
cod fillets on top, browned-side up, and season to taste
with salt and pepper. Cover the casserole and bake for
12–15 minutes, depending on the thickness of the cod,
until it is cooked through and flakes easily.

5 Discard the lemon zest just before serving. Serve the
cod on a bed of the vegetables and sprinkled with
the chopped parsley.

variation
A less expensive fish similar to cod, hake is also ideal to
use in this dish.

156 # trout with mussels and prawns
truite à la dieppoise

Dieppe, on the Normandy coast, is one of France's most important commercial fishing ports, with much of the daily catch going direct to restaurants around the country. Local specialities, indicated by à la dieppoise *in the title, contain mussels, mushrooms and prawns.*

SERVES 4

30 g/1 oz butter

¹/₂ tbsp sunflower oil

12 button mushrooms, thinly sliced

24 live mussels

1 shallot, chopped

1 garlic clove, crushed

250 ml/9 fl oz dry white wine

24 raw prawns in their shells

4 trout fillets, about 175 g/6 oz each, all skin
  and bones removed

250 ml/9 fl oz double cream

salt and pepper

sprigs of fresh chervil, to garnish

for the beurre manié

15 g/¹/₂ oz unsalted butter, softened

15 g/¹/₂ oz plain flour

1 Melt the butter with the oil in a heavy-based frying pan over a medium-high heat. Add the mushrooms and sauté for 5–7 minutes until brown, then set aside.

2 Meanwhile, preheat the oven to 190°C/375°F/Gas Mark 5. Lightly grease an ovenproof dish large enough to hold the trout fillets in a single layer and set aside.

3 To prepare the mussels, cut off and discard any beards, then scrub any dirty shells. Discard any mussels with broken shells or open ones that do not instantly close when tapped.

4 Put the shallot, garlic and wine in a large saucepan with a tight-fitting lid over a high heat and bring to the boil. Reduce the heat to very low. Add the mussels and prawns to the saucepan, cover tightly and simmer for 4 minutes, shaking the pan frequently, or until the mussels open and the prawns turn pink. Discard any mussels that do not open.

5 Line a large sieve with a piece of muslin or kitchen cloth and place over a large bowl. Tip the contents of the pan into the sieve and strain, reserving the cooking liquid.

6 Remove the mussels from their shells, leaving 4 unshelled for a garnish. Peel the prawns and reserve the shells and heads, then set the mussels and prawns aside.

7 Put the cooking liquid in a small saucepan over a high heat, add the prawn shells and heads and boil for 3 minutes, skimming the surface if necessary.

8 Lay the trout fillets in the prepared dish and strain the cooking juices over. Sprinkle with the sliced mushrooms. Cover the dish with foil, shiny-side down, and bake for 10–12 minutes until the trout is tender and flakes easily. Remove the trout, add to the shellfish and cover to keep warm, reserving the cooking liquid.

9 Meanwhile, to make the *beurre manié*, mash the butter and flour together to make a thick paste.

10 To make the sauce, pour the cooking liquid into a small saucepan over a high heat. Bring to the boil, then add in small amounts of the *beurre manié*, whisking constantly and only adding more when the previous amount has been incorporated. Continue boiling and whisking until the sauce is thick and shiny. Stir in the cream and boil until the sauce reduces by half. Add salt and pepper to taste, then stir in the mussels and prawns and just warm through.

11 Transfer the trout fillets to warmed plates and spoon the sauce and shellfish over. Garnish with the chervil and the unshelled mussels.

158
monkfish with courgettes and mushrooms in foil
lotte aux courgettes et champignons en papillote

*The French technique of cooking just about any fish
en papillote, or in a foil parcel, elevates the idea of
one-pot cooking to a higher level – tender seafood,
flavoursome vegetables and a light, fragrant sauce
are ready to serve at once, with plenty of style and
not a lot of washing up.*

SERVES 4

30 g/1 oz unsalted butter, plus extra melted butter
  for greasing the foil

1/2 tbsp sunflower oil

400 g/14 oz button mushrooms, sliced

6 spring onions, finely chopped

2 garlic cloves, very finely chopped

4 tbsp finely chopped fresh flat-leaf parsley

4 centre-cut monkfish fillets, about 175 g/6 oz each

2 tbsp tarragon-flavoured mustard

200 g/7 oz courgettes, very thinly sliced

4 tbsp dry vermouth

salt and pepper

sprigs of fresh flat-leaf parsley, to garnish (optional)

1 Melt the butter with the oil in a heavy-based frying
pan over a medium-high heat. Add the mushrooms
and sauté for 5–7 minutes until brown, then set aside.

2 Meanwhile, preheat the oven to 220°C/425°F/Gas
Mark 7. Mix the spring onions, garlic and chopped
parsley together and set aside. Cut 4 squares of foil
large enough to loosely fold over each piece of
monkfish. Brush the centre of each piece of foil with a
little melted butter.

3 Put a monkfish fillet on a buttered piece of foil and
spread with 1/2 tablespoon of the mustard. Sprinkle
with some of the parsley mixture, then add one-quarter
of the mushrooms and one-quarter of the courgettes.
Sprinkle with 1 tablespoon of dry vermouth and add salt
and pepper to taste.

4 Fold the foil over the fillet and fold the edges
in twice so that none of the juices can escape
during cooking. Repeat to make 3 more parcels.*

5 Place the foil parcels on a baking tray and transfer
to the oven to bake for 10–12 minutes until the fish
flakes easily when you open a parcel to test.

6 To serve, transfer the monkfish and vegetables
to warmed plates and spoon over the juices that
have accumulated in the foil. Garnish with parsley sprigs
to serve, if you like.

*cook's tip

For easy entertaining, the recipe can be prepared
through to the end of Step 4 several hours in advance,
then chilled until 30 minutes before the parcels are put
in the oven. Be sure to bring them to room temperature
before baking.

Overleaf *The Loire Valley provides an abundance of
freshwater fish and delicious white wines to accompany it*

162

marseille-style fish stew
bourride à la marseillaise

SERVES 4–6

large pinch of saffron threads

900 g/2 lb fresh Mediterranean fish, such as sea bass, monkfish, red snapper, haddock, halibut, John Dory or grouper*

24 large raw prawns in their shells

1 squid

2 tbsp olive oil

1 large onion, finely chopped

1 bulb of fennel, thinly sliced, with the feathery green fronds reserved

2 large garlic cloves, crushed

4 tbsp pastis

1 litre/1³/₄ pints Fish Stock

2 large sun-ripened tomatoes, peeled, deseeded and diced, or 400 g/14 oz chopped tomatoes, drained

1 tbsp tomato purée

1 bay leaf

pinch of sugar

pinch of dried chilli flakes (optional)

salt and pepper

French bread, to serve

Every coastal region of France has a local version of fish stew with a varying selection of fish and shellfish. Bouillabaisse is synonymous with harbourside dining in the South of France, but it is only one of the many variations served all along the Mediterranean. The busy port and market in Marseille is one of the largest in France and the neighbouring restaurants feature hearty stews like this.

1 Put the saffron threads in a small dry frying pan over a high heat and toast, stirring constantly, for 1 minute, or until you can smell the aroma. Immediately tip the saffron threads out of the pan and set aside.

2 Prepare the fish, as necessary, removing and reserving all skin, bones and heads. Cut the flesh into large chunks and refrigerate until required. Peel each prawn and remove its head, then slice along its back, from head end to tail end, and use the tip of the knife to remove the dark vein that runs along the back. Refrigerate until required.

3 To prepare the squid, use your fingers to rub off the thin membrane that covers the body. Pull the head and insides out of the body sac, then cut off and reserve the tentacles. Pull out the thin, clear quill that is inside the body. Rinse the squid inside and out, then cut the body into 5-mm/¹/₄-inch rings. Set aside and refrigerate until required.

4 Heat the oil in a large flameproof casserole or heavy-based saucepan over a medium heat. Add the onion and fennel and sauté for 3 minutes, then add the garlic and continue sautéeing for a further 5 minutes, or until the onion and fennel are soft, but not coloured.

5 Remove the casserole from the heat. Warm the pastis in a ladle or small saucepan, ignite and pour it over the onion and fennel to flambé.

6 When the flames die down, return the casserole to the heat and stir in the stock, tomatoes, tomato purée, bay leaf, sugar, chilli flakes, if using, and salt and pepper to taste. Slowly bring to the boil, skimming the surface if necessary, then reduce the heat to low and simmer, uncovered, for 15 minutes. Adjust the seasoning if necessary.

7 Add the prawns and squid rings and simmer just until the prawns turn pink and the squid rings are opaque. Do not overcook or they will be tough. Use a slotted spoon to transfer the prawns and squid rings to serving bowls.

8 Add the fish to the broth and simmer just until the flesh flakes easily, probably not longer than 5 minutes, but it will depend on the type of fish included. Remove smaller, thinner pieces first. Transfer the seafood and broth to the bowls with the prawns and squid and garnish with the reserved fennel fronds. Serve with French bread.

cook's tip

There are not any hard and fast rules about which fish to include – Marseille restaurateurs will rely on the day's catch – but some are more suitable than others. Oily fish, such as mackerel and salmon, should not be included, and swordfish and tuna are considered too 'meaty' for this treatment. Scallops and mussels are also suitable shellfish.

164 skate with brown butter
raie au beurre noisette

For decades this dish appeared on French menus as 'raie au beurre noir', or 'skate with black butter', but now it is more commonly – and more appropriately – described as beurre noisette, *a hazelnut-brown coloured butter, which is the ideal result. Skate's ridged flesh is tender and somewhat gelatinous with a sweet and delicate flavour, and cooking it with the cartilage intact increases the flavour.*

SERVES 2

1 skate wing, about 900 g/2 lb, skinned*

about 1 litre/1³⁄₄ pints Court Bouillon

2 lemon slices

1 bay leaf

55 g/2 oz unsalted butter, chopped

1 tbsp capers in brine, rinsed and dried

1¹⁄₂ tbsp finely chopped fresh flat-leaf parsley

1 tbsp white wine vinegar

salt

lemon wedges, to serve (optional)

1 Put the skate in a large sauté or frying pan or a flameproof casserole large enough to hold it flat. Pour over enough Court Bouillon to cover and add the lemon slices, bay leaf and salt to taste.

2 Slowly bring the liquid to the boil, skimming the surface as necessary, then reduce the heat to low and leave the skate to simmer for 5–7 minutes, or until the flesh easily lifts off the cartilage at the wing's thickest point.

3 Five minutes before the end of the poaching time, melt the butter in a small saucepan over a medium-high heat, just until it turns from yellow to golden brown, but not black.

4 When the fish is poached, transfer it to a warmed platter and use a metal spatula to lift off the top layer of flesh. Lift off the cartilage underneath and discard, then replace the top flesh.

5 Cut the wing in half vertically through the centre, then sprinkle with the capers and parsley.

6 Just as the butter browns, pour it over the skate, then return the saucepan to the heat. Add the vinegar and swirl it around, then pour it over the skate. Serve at immediately with lemon wedges for squeezing over, if you like.

*cook's tip
Always ask the fishmonger to skin the skate as it is very difficult to do at home. If, however, the wings are not skinned, it is easier to do after poaching.

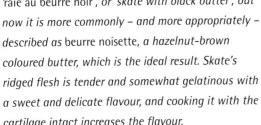

Coastal towns in France rely heavily on tourism and fishing, supplying fresh fish to the rest of France

sole goujons with tartare sauce
sole en goujonnettes sauce tartare

French children and adults alike enjoy these crisp fingers of deep-fried fish. These are served to enjoy with a glass of chilled white wine before dinner or as a main course.

SERVES 4–6

8 sole fillets, about 85 g/3 oz each, all skin
   and bones removed

3–4 tbsp plain flour

85 g/3 oz fine fresh white breadcrumbs

2 large eggs

sunflower oil, for deep-frying

salt and pepper

to serve

Tartare Sauce

lemon wedges

1 Preheat the oven to its lowest temperature. Cut the sole fillets into strips about 7.5 cm/3 inches long and 1 cm/½ inch wide, then set aside.

2 Put the flour with salt and pepper to taste in a polythene bag. Put the breadcrumbs on a flat plate and lightly beat the eggs with salt and pepper to taste in a large flat bowl, such as a soup plate.

3 Heat enough oil for deep-frying in a heavy-based saucepan to 180–190°C/350–375°F, or until a cube of bread browns in 30 seconds. Toss about one-quarter of the fish strips in the seasoned flour, then shake off any excess flour. Quickly dip the fish strips in the egg, then coat with the breadcrumbs, making sure the fish is completely covered.

4 Drop the goujons in the hot oil and deep-fry for 2–3 minutes until golden and crisp. Use a slotted spoon to scoop out the goujons and drain them well on crumpled kitchen paper. Sprinkle with extra salt and keep warm in the oven while frying the remainder, returning the oil to the correct temperature, if necessary, before frying another batch.*

5 Continue until all the fish is fried. Serve with Tartare Sauce on the side and lemon wedges for squeezing.

*cook's tip

It is important to reheat the oil to the correct temperature between batches. If it is too cool, the goujons will not crisp and the breadcrumbs will be greasy; too hot, the breadcrumbs will burn before the fish is cooked.

sole meunière

sole meunière

Rich with melted butter and chopped parsley, this popular seafood dish evokes images of fine French dining, but is very easy for home cooks to prepare. And this version is even easier as it uses sole fillets rather than whole fish that require filleting at the table. New potatoes are the usual accompaniment.

SERVES 2

about 100 ml/3¹/₂ fl oz milk

4 tbsp plain flour

4 sole fillets, about 175 g/6 oz each, all dark skin and
  bones removed

85 g/3 oz Clarified Butter

juice of ¹/₂ lemon

salt and pepper

chopped fresh flat-leaf parsley, to garnish

lemon wedges, to serve

1 Put the milk in a flat dish at least as large as the fillets and put the flour on a plate. Season each fillet on both sides with salt and pepper to taste.

2 Working with 1 fillet at a time, pull it very quickly through the milk, then put it in the flour on both sides and shake off the excess flour. Continue until all the fillets are prepared.

3 Melt half the butter in 1 or 2 sauté or frying pans large enough to hold the fillets in a single layer over a medium-high heat. Add the sole to the pan, skinned-side down, and fry for 2 minutes.

4 Turn the fillets over and fry for 2–3 minutes, or until the flesh flakes easily. Transfer the fish to warmed serving plates, skinned-side up, and reserve.

5 Reduce the heat to medium and melt the remaining butter in the pan. When it stops foaming, squeeze in the lemon juice and stir, scraping the sediment from the base of the pan. Spoon the butter over the soles and sprinkle with the parsley. Serve with lemon wedges.

variation

Dover sole, with its delicate and flavoursome flesh, is the fish of choice for French chefs, but lemon sole is an acceptable, less expensive alternative. Other flatfish, such as plaice or flounder, also work well in this recipe.

168
tuna with green sauce
thon sauce verte

This versatile dish of sizzling hot tuna and a cool piquant sauce from the picturesque town of Menton, nestling on the Mediterranean between Monaco and Italy, tastes equally good after the tuna has been left to cool. An ideal dish for summer entertaining.

SERVES 4

4 fresh tuna steaks, about 2 cm/³/₄ inch thick

olive oil

salt and pepper

*for the Green Sauce**

55 g/2 oz fresh flat-leaf parsley, leaves and stems

4 spring onions, chopped

2 garlic cloves, chopped

3 anchovy fillets in oil, drained

30 g/1 oz fresh basil leaves

¹/₂ tbsp capers in brine, rinsed and dried

2 sprigs of fresh oregano or ¹/₂ tsp dried oregano

125 ml/4 fl oz extra-virgin olive oil, plus extra for
  brushing the tuna

1–2 tbsp lemon juice, to taste

1 To make the Green Sauce, put the parsley, spring onions, garlic, anchovy fillets, basil, capers and oregano in a food processor. Pulse to chop and blend together. With the motor still running, pour in the oil through the feed tube. Add lemon juice to taste, then whiz again. If the sauce is too thick, add a little extra oil. Cover and chill until required.

2 Place a ridged cast-iron frying pan over a high heat until you can feel the heat rising from the surface. Brush the tuna steaks with oil and place, oiled-side down, on the hot pan and chargrill for 2 minutes.

3 Lightly brush the top side of the tuna steaks with a little more oil. Use a pair of tongs to turn the tuna steaks over, then season to taste with salt and pepper. Continue chargrilling for a further 2 minutes for rare or up to 4 minutes for well done.

4 Transfer the tuna steaks to serving plates and serve with the Green Sauce spooned over.

*cook's tip
The Green Sauce can be made up to a day in advance and chilled in a covered container in the refrigerator. Pour a thin layer of oil over the top of the sauce to preserve the colour. The oil can be stirred in before serving.

grilled red mullet with fennel and peppers

rouget grillé aux poivrons et fenouil

For a meal with a Provençal feel, serve this dish with toasted slices of French bread spread with Tapenade on the side.

SERVES 4

6 red mullet fillets, about 125 g/4$^{1}/_{2}$ oz each, scaled*

4 tbsp olive oil

2 large red peppers, deseeded and thinly sliced

2 bulbs of fennel, thinly sliced

2 large garlic cloves, crushed

salt and pepper

lemon wedges, to serve

1 Pick over the mullet fillets and use a pair of tweezers to remove the fine bones running along the centre of each fillet.

2 Heat 2 tablespoons of the oil in a large sauté or frying pan with a tight-fitting lid over a medium-high heat. Add the peppers, fennel and garlic and stir around. Add salt and pepper to taste, then reduce the heat to medium-low, cover the pan and leave the vegetables to cook for 15–20 minutes until soft.

3 Meanwhile, preheat the grill to high. When the grill is very, very hot, brush the skin of the fillets with oil and season to taste with salt and pepper. Put the fillets on a baking tray, skin-side up, and grill for 3 minutes, or until the skin crisps and becomes golden brown.

4 Turn the fillets over, brush again with a little oil and season to taste with salt and pepper. Continue to grill for a minute or so until the flesh flakes easily when tested with the tip of a knife.

5 Divide the fennel and peppers between 4 plates. Cut each fillet in half and arrange 3 pieces on top of each portion of the vegetables. Serve immediately with lemon wedges for squeezing over.

*cook's tip

Scaling fish is a messy business, so it is best to ask the fishmonger to do it. If you do it yourself, however, put the fish inside a polythene bag as you work to prevent the scales flying all over the kitchen.

170 scallops with breadcrumbs and parsley
coquilles st jacques à la provençale

Scallops are expensive, so it is important that they are quickly cooked for their delicate, sweet flesh to be appreciated. This simple-looking, but very rich, dish is served in the numerous seafood restaurants that surround Nice's colourful flower market.

SERVES 4

20 large fresh scallops, removed from their shells,
    about 4 cm/1½ inches thick*

200 g/7 oz Clarified Butter

85 g/3 oz day-old French bread, made into
    fine breadcrumbs

4 garlic cloves, finely chopped

5 tbsp finely chopped fresh flat-leaf parsley

salt and pepper

lemon wedges, to serve

The beauty of Mont-St-Michel draws many tourists to cross the causeway that links it to the mainland

1 Preheat the oven to its lowest temperature. Use a small knife to remove the dark vein that runs around each scallop, then rinse and pat dry. Season to taste with salt and pepper and set aside.

2 Melt half the butter in a large sauté or frying pan over a high heat. Add the breadcrumbs, reduce the heat to medium and fry, stirring, for 5–6 minutes until they are golden brown and crisp. Remove the breadcrumbs from the pan and drain well on kitchen paper, then keep warm in the oven. Wipe out the pan.

3 Use 2 large sauté or frying pans to cook all the scallops at once without overcrowding the pans. Melt 50 g/1¾ oz of the butter in each pan over a high heat. Reduce the heat to medium, divide the scallops between the 2 pans in single layers and fry for 2 minutes.

4 Turn the scallops over and continue frying for a further 2–3 minutes until they are golden and cooked through if you cut one with a knife. Add extra butter to the pans if necessary.

5 Divide the scallops between 4 warmed plates and sprinkle with the breadcrumbs and parsley mixed together. Serve with lemon wedges for squeezing over.

*cook's tip
Because fresh scallops come in varying thicknesses, it is important to buy similar sizes so that they all cook in the same time and some don't overcook and become tough. If you've never cooked scallops before, buy an extra 1 or 2 to practise the timing. A well-cooked scallop will be golden brown, slightly resistant when pressed and opaque when cut open. Scallops 2.5 cm/1 inch thick, for example, will only need about 90 seconds cooking in Step 4.

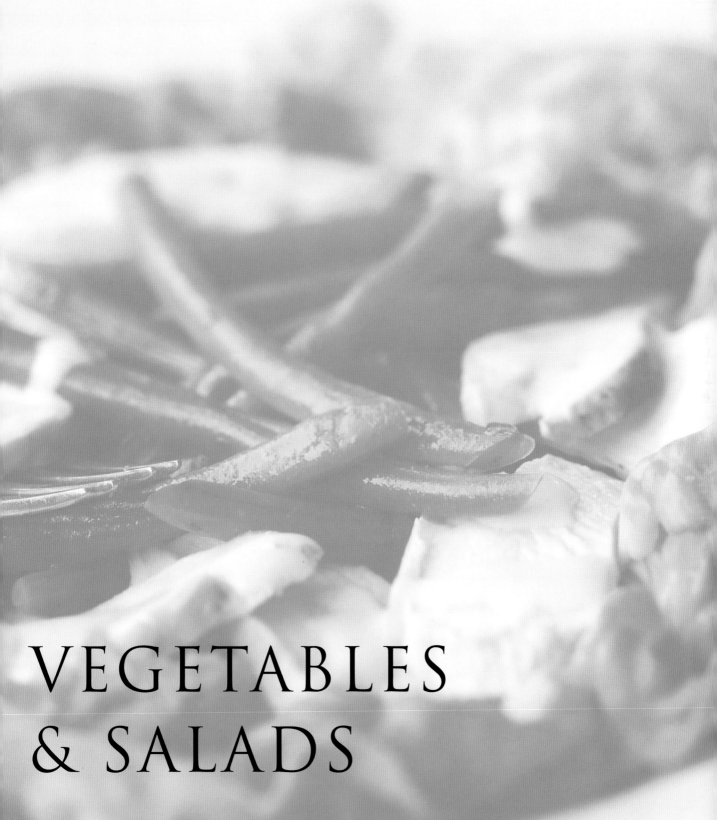

VEGETABLES
& SALADS

174 French cooks are fortunate to have a year-round supply of fantastic-looking seasonal vegetables to choose from. A walk past the vegetable stalls in French markets and through the fresh produce departments of French supermarkets often turns cooks from other countries green with envy. Whatever the season, vegetables – and fresh fruit – are attractively displayed, appealing to the eye as much as to the palate. Even small corner shopkeepers take great care when setting out their produce.

Fresh vegetables are an important part of French cooking, but not in the 'meat-and-two-veg' tradition of Anglo-Saxon countries. One of the great mysteries for many foreigners visiting France for the first time, especially when they are eating only in restaurants, is where all the perfect-looking vegetables have gone. Much of French vegetable cooking takes place in French homes. Large portions of plainly cooked vegetables, say carrots or turnips, are not traditionally served as part of French restaurant meals. Instead, vegetables are incorporated into the main dishes (*plats principaux*), such as the tiny onions and button mushrooms in a classic Beef Bourguignon (see page 108) or the baby turnips, new potatoes and tender young peas in Spring Lamb Stew (see page 118). When plain vegetables are served, such as green beans (*haricots verts*), it will be on a separate plate.

French restaurant dishes are prepared with 'vegetable garnishes' (*garniture*), which to non-cooks simply means the vegetables cooked with the main course. Dishes described on a menu as '*à la parisienne*', for example, will contain small fried potato balls tossed with finely chopped parsley. '*A la florentine*' is with spinach and '*à la forestière*' is with wild mushrooms, usually with potatoes and bacon. After a few days of restaurant dining, if a craving for a large quantity of vegetables develops, ask for *haricots verts*, which are almost always available blanched and seasoned.

The potato, *pomme de terre* or literally 'apple of the earth', is undoubtedly the most popular French vegetable. Sautéed Potatoes (see page 183) are a regular accompaniment to pan-fried or grilled steaks and chops, often served without being ordered. In the Dordogne, the humble sautéed spuds are cooked with goose fat and elevated to luxury status with the generous addition of truffles in *pommes de terre à la sarladaise*. From Lyon, Potatoes and Onions (see page 194) also makes a meal out of a quickly cooked piece of meat. France's best-known potato dish, however, has to be the ultra-rich Potato and Cheese Gratin (see page 192) from the Dauphiné region around Grenoble, in which thin slices of potato are slowly simmered in double cream with a hint of nutmeg. The golden-brown melted cheese topping makes this an irresistible dish, a natural match for roast leg of lamb (*gigot d'agneau*).

The large market gardens of northern France send their supplies to Rungis, the massive wholesale market outside Paris that services the capital's chefs. Brittany, the Loire Valley, the Rhône Valley and Provence also produce everything that French chefs

require. Every summer in the south, Provençal market stalls become tourist attractions in themselves with their colourful produce. Globe artichokes (*artichauts*), aubergines (*aubergines*), beetroots (*betteraves*), courgettes (*courgettes*), red and green peppers (*poivrons rouges et verts*) and tomatoes (*tomates*) are piled high along with bunches of sunflowers, huge garlic bulbs and mixed salad leaves. The vegetarian stew Ratatouille (see page 180) is like a market stall in a pot. To add the summer flavours of southern France to any meal, try Artichokes with Vierge Sauce (see page 184) or Stuffed Tomatoes (see page 187).

In such a meat-eating country as France, vegetarians can be presented with menus with few options. Salvation, however, often comes in the form of arranged salads (*salades composée*). French cooks excel at combining raw and cooked ingredients to make salads that are meals in themselves. Salad Niçoise (see page 196), with tuna, blanched beans, tomatoes, olives and anchovies, is the best-known, enjoyed around the world. When served with a glass of chilled rosé wine, a Salad Niçoise represents the best of summer eating. Grilled Pepper Salad (see page 198) is another summer dish that doesn't make many demands on the cook. Grilled Goat's Cheese Salad (see page 201) and Mixed Leaves with Warm Chicken Livers (see page 200) are examples of bistro salads. And, for a taste of Paris café society, try Les Deux Magots Salad (see page 199). It's similar to the one sold around the clock at the legendary stylish Saint-Germain-des-Prés café, with poached chicken in a lightly curried dressing and blanched green beans.

Previous page *A modest-sized basket is all that's required if you shop as the locals do – on a daily basis*

Artists such as Cézanne, Monet and Picasso drew much
of their inspiration from French coastal areas

178
asparagus with hollandaise sauce
asperges sauce hollandaise

It is as if all France celebrates when asparagus comes into season in April. It features on menus du jour from cafés to Michelin-starred restaurants. Market stalls pile it high and roadside stalls sell it at farm gates. French asparagus is white with pale purple tips and the thicker the stalk, the more it is valued, with the most expensive being about as thick as a thumb. The cooking technique is the same as for green asparagus – cook it upright in boiling water so that the tips steam and don't become overcooked before the stalks are tender. A stainless-steel asparagus cooker, with an internal wire basket, is a good investment if you cook lots of asparagus, but a deep ordinary saucepan will work just fine.

SERVES 4

650 g/1 lb 7 oz white or green asparagus

for the Hollandaise Sauce

4 tbsp white wine vinegar

¹/₂ tbsp finely chopped shallot

5 black peppercorns

1 bay leaf

3 large egg yolks

140 g/5 oz unsalted butter, finely diced

2 tsp lemon juice

pinch of cayenne pepper

2 tbsp single cream (optional)

salt

1 Whether you are using white or green asparagus, break off any woody ends of the stems. Trim the stalks so that they are all the same height. Use a small knife or vegetable peeler to remove the stringy fibres from the white asparagus, trimming from the tip towards the end.

2 Bring a kettle of water to the boil. Divide the asparagus into 4 bundles and use kitchen string to tie the bundles together, criss-crossing the string from just below the tips to the base so that the bundles can stand upright.

3 Stand the bundles upright in the deepest saucepan you have. Pour in enough water to come about three-quarters of the way up the stalks and then cover them with a loose tent of foil, shiny-side down, inside the pan.

4 Heat the water in the saucepan until bubbles appear around the side of the pan, then continue simmering for 10 minutes, or until the stalks are just tender when pierced with the tip of a knife.

5 Meanwhile, to make the Hollandaise Sauce, put the vinegar, shallot, peppercorns and bay leaf in a small saucepan over a high heat and boil until reduced to 1 tablespoon. Leave to cool slightly, then strain into a heatproof bowl that will fit over a saucepan of simmering water without the bowl touching the water.

6 Beat the egg yolks into the reduced vinegar mixture. Set the bowl over the saucepan of simmering water and whisk the egg yolks constantly until the yolks are thick enough to leave a trail on the surface. Do not let the water boil.

7 Gradually beat in the pieces of butter, piece by piece, whisking constantly until the sauce is like soft mayonnaise.* Stir in the lemon juice, then add salt to taste and the cayenne pepper. Stir in the cream for a richer taste, if desired. Transfer to 4 small serving bowls.

8 Drain the asparagus well. Untie the bundles and arrange the spears on individual plates. Serve immediately with the bowls of Hollandaise Sauce. To eat, pick up the asparagus, stalk by stalk, and dip the tips in the hot sauce.

*cook's tip

When making the sauce, take care only to add a piece of butter after the previous piece is incorporated. This should prevent the sauce from curdling or separating. If it does curdle or separate, however, beat an extra egg yolk in a separate bowl. Slowly add in the curdled mixture, whisking constantly, and the sauce should become smooth again.

182

french-style peas
petits pois à la française

More than half of France's peas are grown in the north of the country, but the phrase à la française *in the title is a clue that lets anyone know this simple preparation is eaten throughout the country. Try these with a simple Old-fashioned Roast Chicken.*

SERVES 4–6

1.3 kg/3 lb fresh peas, shelled, or 450 g/1 lb frozen peas

1 head of lettuce, core removed, shredded

4 shallots, chopped

1 Bouquet Garni

125 g/4$\frac{1}{2}$ oz butter, diced

1 tbsp caster sugar

2–4 tbsp water

salt and pepper

1 Put the peas, lettuce, shallots, Bouquet Garni, butter, sugar and salt and pepper to taste in a heavy-based saucepan with a tight-fitting lid or a flameproof casserole over a medium-high heat. Stir in 4 tablespoons of water if using fresh peas and 2 tablespoons of water if using frozen peas.

2 Slowly bring to the boil and stir, then reduce the heat to low, cover the pan tightly and simmer for 10–20 minutes until the peas are tender and the liquid is absorbed.*

3 Adjust the seasoning if necessary, then transfer to a warmed serving dish and serve.

*cook's tip

If the peas are tender in Step 2 before all the liquid is absorbed, remove the lid and cook over a high heat, stirring, until the excess water evaporates.

sautéed potatoes

pommes de terre sautées

Sautéeing potatoes is second nature to many French cooks and this preparation is what is most often served with simply grilled meat and chops.

SERVES 4–6

900 g/2 lb waxy potatoes, such as Charlotte, peeled
  and cut into chunks

55 g/2 oz Clarified Butter

salt and pepper

chopped fresh flat-leaf parsley or spring onions,
  to garnish

1 Bring a large saucepan of salted water to the boil over a high heat. Add the potatoes and, as soon as the water returns to the boil, drain them well. Pat the potatoes completely dry.

2 Melt the butter in a large sauté or frying pan with a tight-fitting lid over a medium-high heat. You only want a thin layer of butter, about 3 mm/⅛ inch deep, so, depending on the size of the pan, pour off and reserve any excess.

3 Add the potatoes and sauté for 4 minutes, rolling them around the pan, until they are golden all over. Add a little of the reserved butter, if necessary.

4 Reduce the heat to very low, cover the pan tightly and leave the potatoes to cook for 15–20 minutes, shaking the pan occasionally, until they are golden brown and do not offer any resistance when you pierce them with a knife. Add salt and pepper to taste, then stir in the parsley.

variation

Sautéeing potatoes in butter gives them a rich flavour, but ordinary butter would probably burn in Step 3 before it becomes hot enough to crisp up the potatoes. This is why Clarified Butter is specified, as it can be heated to a higher temperature without burning. If you don't have any, use 40 g/1½ oz unsalted butter with 1 tablespoon sunflower oil. The addition of oil lets the butter reach a higher temperature without burning.

184

artichokes with vierge sauce
artichauts au sauce vierge

Artichokes have been a firm favourite with the French since Catherine de' Medici introduced them to the country from Italy. The name of this sauce translates as 'virgin sauce', referring to the fact that it is made with extra-virgin olive oil.

SERVES 4

4 large globe artichokes

¹/₂ lemon, sliced

for the Vierge Sauce

3 large beef tomatoes, peeled, deseeded and finely diced

4 spring onions, very finely chopped

6 tbsp chopped fresh herbs, such as basil, chervil, chives, mint, flat-leaf parsley or tarragon

150 ml/5 fl oz full-flavoured extra-virgin olive oil

pinch of sugar

salt and pepper

1 To prepare the artichokes, cut off the stems and trim the base of each so that it will stand upright on the plate. Use scissors to snip off the leaf tips, then drop each artichoke in a bowl of water with 2 of the lemon slices while the others are being prepared.

2 Meanwhile, select a saucepan large enough to hold the 4 artichokes upright and half-fill with salted water and the remaining lemon slices. Bring the water to the boil, add the artichokes and place a heatproof plate on top to keep them submerged. Reduce the heat to a low boil and continue boiling the artichokes for 25–35 minutes, depending on size, until the bottom leaves easily pull out.

3 While the artichokes are cooking, prepare the Vierge Sauce. Put the tomatoes, spring onions, herbs, oil, sugar and salt and pepper to taste in a saucepan and set aside for the flavours to blend.

4 When the artichokes are tender, drain them upside down on kitchen paper, then transfer to individual plates. Heat the sauce very gently until it is just warm, then spoon it equally over the artichokes.

variation
Artichokes are also often served with a small bowl of sauce on the side for dipping the leaves into. Other suitable sauces include Hollandaise Sauce, Vinaigrette or Garlic Vinaigrette.

Good food – both in restaurants and shops – can be found off the beaten track, as well as in the large towns

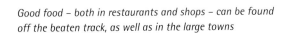

186

vichy carrots
carottes à la vichyssoise

Carrots are one of the major crops in the agricultural region around Vichy, but the spa town is perhaps better known for its bottled water from thermal springs, exported around the world. Originally, this glazed carrot dish is said to have been prepared by adding bicarbonate of soda and sugar to the cooking water, but bottled water is more often used today to capture the same flavour.

SERVES 4–6

2 tbsp unsalted butter

450 g/1 lb carrots, peeled and cut into
  5-mm/¼-inch slices

1 tbsp sugar

bottle of Vichy mineral water*

salt and pepper

2 tbsp chopped fresh flat-leaf parsley, to garnish

1 Melt the butter in a large heavy-based saucepan over a medium-high heat. Stir in the carrots, then stir in the sugar and salt and pepper to taste.

2 Pour over enough Vichy water to cover the carrots by 5 cm/2 inches and bring to the boil. Reduce the heat to medium and leave the carrots to simmer, uncovered, stirring occasionally, until they are tender, all the liquid has been absorbed and they are coated in a thin glaze.

3 Adjust the seasoning if necessary, transfer to a serving dish and stir in the parsley to garnish.

*cook's tip
If you don't have bottled Vichy water, add 1 teaspoon bicarbonate of soda to the cooking water with the sugar.

stuffed tomatoes
tomates à la provençale

1 Preheat the oven to 190°C/375°F/Gas Mark 5 and lightly grease 1 or 2 shallow ovenproof dishes that will hold the tomato halves upright without them touching. Cut each tomato in half crossways, then use a teaspoon to scoop out the seeds.

2 Combine the breadcrumbs, parsley, basil, garlic and salt and pepper to taste in a large bowl and drizzle just a little oil over to moisten. Divide the stuffing equally between the tomato halves, mounding it slightly in the centre of each.

3 Drizzle a little extra oil over the top of the tomatoes. Place the tomatoes in the oven and bake for 20–25 minutes until they are tender, but still holding their shape, and the stuffing is crisp. Serve immediately or leave to cool completely and serve at room temperature, with the salad leaves tossed in vinaigrette on the side.

*cook's tip
At the height of summer, when bright red tomatoes are at their best, their flesh will not collapse during cooking. During the rest of the year, however, when hot-house tomatoes are the only option, sprinkle the inside of the tomato halves with salt and leave to drain upside down on kitchen paper for 20 minutes to remove the excess water from the flesh.

When summer arrives in Provence and tomatoes are at their most flavoursome, this simple dish appears on menus everywhere. Expect to taste garlic and tomatoes when a recipe has à la provençale *in the title. These can be served hot or prepared in advance and served at room temperature to avoid cooking in the heat of the afternoon or early evening.*

SERVES 4

4 large, sun-ripened tomatoes*

85 g/3 oz fine fresh white breadcrumbs

55 g/2 oz fresh flat-leaf parsley, stems and leaves, very finely chopped

1 tbsp finely torn fresh basil leaves

4 large garlic cloves, very finely chopped

3–4 tbsp fruity extra-virgin olive oil

salt and pepper

to serve

mixed salad leaves

Garlic Vinaigrette

188 courgette and cheese gratin
gratin de courgettes

There aren't many French home cooks who don't have a favourite gratin recipe in their repertoire. These are simple vegetable dishes with a bubbling golden topping that are easily adapted to whatever looks best in the market. Although often made with potatoes, this recipe is an example of a lighter custard-based gratin. This dish goes particularly well with roast lamb.

SERVES 4–6

55 g/2 oz unsalted butter

6 courgettes, sliced

2 tbsp chopped fresh tarragon or a mixture of mint,
   tarragon and flat-leaf parsley

200 g/7 oz Gruyère or Parmesan cheese, grated

125 ml/4 fl oz milk

125 ml/4 fl oz double cream

2 eggs

freshly grated nutmeg

salt and pepper

1 Preheat the oven to 180°C/350°F/Gas Mark 4. Grease an ovenproof serving dish and set aside.

2 Melt the butter in a large sauté or frying pan over a medium-high heat. Add the courgettes and sauté for 4–6 minutes, turning the slices over occasionally, until coloured on both sides. Remove from the pan and drain on kitchen paper, then season to taste with salt and pepper.

3 Spread half the courgettes over the base of the dish. Sprinkle with half the herbs and 85 g/3 oz of the cheese. Repeat these layers once more.

4 Mix the milk, cream and eggs together and add nutmeg and salt and pepper to taste. Pour this liquid over the courgettes, then sprinkle the top with the remaining cheese.

5 Bake the gratin for 35–45 minutes until it is set in the centre and golden brown. Remove from the oven and leave to stand for 5 minutes before serving straight from the dish.

Above *The vibrant colour of the French countryside is a visual feast for the eyes of its many visitors*

Overleaf *Markets such as this one in Nice are packed with a huge selection of wonderful fresh produce grown locally*

potato and cheese gratin
pommes dauphine

192

Dauphiné is a little-known region of southeastern France around Grenoble, but it has given its name to this rich dish, which is probably France's best-known gratin. The use of cream in this recipe is typical of the region's cuisine.

SERVES 4–6

900 g/2 lb waxy potatoes, such as Charlotte, peeled and thinly sliced

1 large garlic clove, halved

225 ml/8 fl oz double cream

freshly grated nutmeg

175 g/6 oz Gruyère cheese, finely grated

butter, for greasing and dotting over the top

salt and pepper

1 Preheat the oven to 190°C/375°F/Gas Mark 5. Put the potato slices in a bowl, cover with cold water and leave to stand for 5 minutes, then drain well.

2 Meanwhile, rub the base and sides of a 1.4-litre/2¹⁄₂-pint oval gratin or ovenproof dish with the cut sides of the garlic halves, pressing down firmly to impart the flavour. Lightly grease the sides of the dish with butter.

3 Place the potatoes in a bowl with the cream and season to taste with freshly grated nutmeg and salt and pepper. Use your hands to mix everything together, then transfer the potatoes to the gratin dish and pour over any cream remaining in the bowl.

4 Sprinkle the cheese over the top and dot with butter. Place the gratin dish on a baking tray and bake for 60–80 minutes until the potatoes are tender when pierced with a skewer and the top is golden and bubbling.* Leave to stand for about 2 minutes, then serve straight from the gratin dish.

*cook's tip

If the top of the gratin begins to brown too much before the potatoes are tender, cover it with a sheet of foil, shiny-side down.

Fountains and water features cool the squares and other public places of many French towns and cities

194 # potatoes and onions
pommes de terre à la lyonnaise

Lyon is one of the gourmet centres of France and recipes labelled à la lyonnaise *come from the region and usually contain onions. This dish, with the characteristic onions, is excellent to serve with roast and grilled meats.*

SERVES 4–6

700 g/1 lb 9 oz waxy potatoes, such as Charlotte, scrubbed

115 g/4 oz Clarified Butter

2 onions, thinly sliced

1 garlic clove, finely chopped

2 tbsp finely chopped fresh flat-leaf parsley

salt and pepper

1 Preheat the oven to 200°C/400°F/Gas Mark 6. Put the unpeeled potatoes in a large saucepan of salted water and bring to the boil over a high heat. Boil for 7–10 minutes, or until just tender. Drain well, and when cool enough to handle, peel and cut into 5-mm/¼-inch slices.

2 Melt half the Clarified Butter in a large ovenproof sauté pan or frying pan over a medium-high heat. Add the onions and sauté for 5 minutes, or until softened and pale golden, then add the garlic and continue sautéeing for 2 minutes, but do not let the onion brown. Remove from the pan and reserve.

3 Add the potato slices, working in batches if necessary, and fry for 4 minutes on each side, adding the remaining Clarified Butter as necessary. Remove two-thirds of the potatoes from the pan with a slotted spoon.

4 Spread the potatoes remaining in the pan over the base. Add half the onions and season to taste with salt and pepper. Top with half the remaining potatoes, the remaining onion and salt and pepper to taste. Cover with the remaining potatoes and season.

5 Transfer the pan to the oven and bake for 10–15 minutes until the top is golden brown. Sprinkle with the parsley and serve.

braised chicory
endives braisées

This simple technique of braising the pearly white chicory in butter with a little sugar helps to counter the naturally bitter taste. This is ideal to serve with steaks or Roast Chicken with Salad.

SERVES 4

4 large heads of chicory

30 g/1 oz unsalted butter

¹/₂ lemon

2 tsp sugar

salt and pepper

1 Cut off the loose yellow tip of each head of chicory, then remove any outer leaves that are bruised or have brown spots. Cut each head in half lengthways, then use the tip of the knife to cut out the cores.

2 Melt the butter in a large sauté or frying pan that will hold the chicory halves in a single layer. Add the chicory, rounded-side down, and leave to fry for 2 minutes until they are golden brown on that side.

3 Turn the chicory halves over and squeeze a little lemon juice over them. Sprinkle the chicory halves with the sugar and salt and pepper to taste, and continue cooking for 3–5 minutes until golden brown on the cut sides and the heads feel tender when you pierce them with the tip of a knife or a skewer.

196 salad niçoise
salade niçoise

Ask ten French chefs for a salade niçoise *recipe and you'll get ten versions – each different and each described as* the most authentic, traditional recipe. *It might be a matter of debate in culinary circles as to whether this Mediterranean salad should contain tomatoes, green beans or hard-boiled eggs, but inevitably most salads contain all.*

SERVES 4–6 AS A MAIN COURSE

2 tuna steaks, about 2 cm/³/₄ inch thick

olive oil

250 g/9 oz French beans, topped and tailed

1 quantity Garlic Vinaigrette

2 hearts of lettuce, leaves separated

3 large hard-boiled eggs, quartered*

2 juicy vine-ripened tomatoes, cut into wedges

50 g/1³/₄ oz anchovy fillets in oil, drained

55 g/2 oz Niçoise olives

salt and pepper

torn fresh basil leaves, to garnish

French bread, to serve

1 Heat a ridged cast-iron griddle pan over a high heat until you can feel the heat rising from the surface. Brush the tuna steaks with oil, place, oiled-side down, on the hot pan and chargrill for 2 minutes.

2 Lightly brush the top side of the tuna steaks with a little more oil. Use a pair of tongs to turn the tuna steaks over, then season to taste with salt and pepper. Continue chargrilling for a further 2 minutes for rare or up to 4 minutes for well done. Leave to cool.

3 Meanwhile, bring a saucepan of salted water to the boil. Add the beans to the pan and return to the boil, then boil for 3 minutes, or until tender-crisp. Drain the beans and immediately transfer them to a large bowl. Pour over the Garlic Vinaigrette and stir together, then leave the beans to cool in the dressing.

4 To serve, line a platter with lettuce leaves. Lift the beans out of the bowl, leaving the excess dressing behind, and pile them in the centre of the platter. Break the tuna into large flakes and arrange it over the beans.

5 Arrange the hard-boiled eggs and tomatoes around the side. Place the anchovy fillets over the salad, then scatter with the olives and basil. Drizzle the remaining dressing in the bowl over everything and serve with plenty of French bread for mopping up the dressing.

*cook's tip

To hard-boil the eggs, place them in a saucepan and pour over enough boiling water to cover. Return to the boil, then boil for 10 minutes. Drain the eggs and leave them under cold running water to stop them cooking, then shell. The unshelled eggs can be stored in the refrigerator for up to a week, but if stored for longer, a thin green line will develop between the yolk and white. Freshly boiled eggs have much more flavour and colour.

198

grilled pepper salad
salade de poivrons grillés

This is the quintessential Mediterranean salad. Hot-house peppers are sold all year round, but this salad is at its best in summer when the sweet, crisp peppers are piled high on market stalls. A mixture of peppers looks attractive, but using all red or all yellow peppers will be just as flavoursome. This is an excellent salad to serve alongside Chicken with 40 Cloves of Garlic or a roast leg of lamb.

SERVES 4 AS A MAIN COURSE

2 red peppers

2 green peppers

2 yellow or orange peppers

125 ml/4 fl oz Vinaigrette or Herb Vinaigrette

6 spring onions, finely chopped

1 tbsp capers in brine, rinsed

200 g/7 oz soft goat's cheese, any rind removed

chopped fresh flat-leaf parsley, to serve

1 Preheat the grill to high. Arrange the peppers on a grill pan, position about 10 cm/4 inches from the heat and grill for 8–10 minutes, turning them frequently, until the skins are charred all over. Transfer the peppers to a bowl, cover with a damp tea towel and leave to stand until cool enough to handle.

2 Using a small knife, peel each of the peppers. Working over a bowl to catch the juices from inside the peppers, cut each pepper in half and remove the cores and seeds, then cut the flesh into thin strips.

3 Arrange the peppers on a serving platter and spoon over the reserved juices, then add the dressing. Sprinkle over the spring onions and capers, then crumble over the cheese. If not serving immediately, cover and chill until required. Sprinkle with the parsley, to serve.

les deux magots salad

salade les deux magots

This salad is an example of the composed salads, or salades composées, *which are so popular with the French. With the lightly curried dressing, this is similar to one of the signature dishes on the menu at the fashionable café Les Deux Magots on Boulevard St-Germain, in the Left Bank district of Paris. It is served throughout the day and into the early hours of the morning. The café takes its name from the two wooden statues of Chinese commercial agents, or* magots, *that watch over the dining room and the bustling waiters with their black bow ties and jackets and crisp long white aprons.*

SERVES 4–6 AS A MAIN COURSE

450 g/1 lb French beans, topped and tailed

150 ml/5 fl oz Herb Vinaigrette

200 g/7 oz Mayonnaise

$^1\!/_2$ tbsp lemon juice, or to taste

$^1\!/_2$ tsp korma curry paste, or to taste

$^1\!/_2$ tsp ground turmeric

single cream (optional)

2 hearts of lettuce, leaves separated

3 cooked chicken breasts, skinned and thinly sliced
  on the diagonal

salt and pepper

1 Bring a large saucepan of salted water to the boil and put iced water in a large bowl. Add the beans to the boiling water, return to the boil and continue boiling for 5 minutes, or until the beans are tender. Drain them, then immediately plunge them into the iced water to stop the cooking and leave to cool completely.

2 When the beans are cool, drain them well and pat dry, then toss with the Herb Vinaigrette and reserve.

3 Meanwhile, to make the curry-flavoured dressing, place the Mayonnaise in a bowl and beat until smooth. Add the lemon juice, curry paste and turmeric and stir together. Stir in the cream, if using, until the dressing has a thin pouring consistency. Taste and add extra lemon juice or curry paste, if desired, and salt and pepper to taste. Cover and chill until required.

4 To serve, line a serving platter or individual plates with the lettuce leaves. Place the dressed beans in the centre of the platter or plates. Arrange the chicken slices around the beans, slightly overlapping, then drizzle the curry-flavoured dressing over the chicken.

mixed leaves with warm chicken livers
salade tiède de foie de volaille

200

'Tiède' translates as 'lukewarm' and this is an example of the popular French style of serving warm ingredients with dressed salad leaves. Bistro menus often feature salades tièdes.

SERVES 4 AS A MAIN COURSE

250 g/9 oz mixed salad leaves, large ones torn into bite-sized pieces*

2 tbsp chopped fresh flat-leaf parsley

2 tbsp snipped fresh chives

3–4 tbsp olive oil

100 g/3½ oz shallots, finely chopped

1 large garlic clove, finely chopped

500 g/1 lb 2 oz chicken livers, cored, trimmed and halved

3 tbsp raspberry vinegar

salt and pepper

French bread, to serve

1 Toss the salad leaves with the parsley and chives and divide between individual plates.

2 Heat 2 tablespoons of the oil in a sauté or frying pan over a medium-high heat. Add the shallots and garlic and sauté for 2 minutes, or until the shallots are soft, but not brown.

3 Add an extra tablespoon of the oil to the sauté pan and heat. Add the chicken livers and sauté for 5 minutes, or until they are just pink in the centre when you cut one in half. Add a little extra oil to the pan while the chicken livers are sautéing, if necessary.

4 Increase the heat to high, add the raspberry vinegar and quickly stir around. Season to taste with salt and pepper, then spoon the livers and cooking juices over the mixed leaves. Serve immediately with French bread.

*cook's tip

French cooks have long been used to going to a market and purchasing *mesclun*, a mixture of fresh bitter and sweet salad leaves for their salads. To replicate an authentic French bistro flavour, buy a bag of mixed leaves that includes lamb's lettuce and rocket. Fresh cress, escarole, curly endive, oak-leaf lettuce and young spinach leaves are also ideal to include.

grilled goat's cheese salad
salade de chèvre

A bistro favourite that fits the bill for lunch or a light meal at any time of the day. French goat's cheese comes in numerous shapes, sizes and flavours – always try to taste before buying to avoid buying one that is too harsh for your palette. Crottin de chavignol, *from the Loire valley, for example, will hold its shape during grilling after the top and bottom rind are thinly cut off.*

SERVES 4

12 slices French bread

175 g/6 oz round goat's cheese in a log, cut into
  12 slices

125 g/4^1/$_2$ oz mixed salad leaves, large ones torn into
  bite-sized pieces

2 tbsp snipped fresh chives

6 tbsp Vinaigrette or Garlic Vinaigrette

pepper

1 Preheat the grill to high. Place the bread slices on a grill rack and toast the bread slices until crisp and golden, but not dark brown. Immediately remove the grill rack from under the grill and turn the slices of toast over.

2 Place a slice of goat's cheese on each bread slice, then return them to the grill and grill for 2 minutes, or until the cheese is golden and bubbling.

3 Meanwhile, place the salad leaves in a large bowl with the chives, add the dressing of choice and use your hands to toss until the leaves are coated.

4 Divide the salad between individual plates, top each with 3 cheese-topped toasts and serve while still hot, seasoned with black pepper to taste.

DESSERTS

204 The French dessert repertoire ranges lusciously from the sublime, extravagant and sophisticated to the very, very simple. Chocolate is popular, but fresh fruits, custard, spices, caramel and vanilla all have starring roles as well. The complex, labour-intensive creations of *haute cuisine* restaurants, such as elaborate cakes (*gâteaux*), however, are best left to the professionals, and nobody is more in agreement with this sentiment than the average French home cook, who buys special desserts when an occasion calls for pushing out the boat.

Velvety smooth Crème Brûlée, with its thin layer of crisp caramel that has to be cracked to reach the set custard underneath, is one of the best-loved French desserts, by the French and Francophiles alike. Traditionally, Crème Brûlée is flavoured with vanilla, with the tiny seeds studding the set creamy custard, but Espresso Crème Brûlée (see page 210) is an example of a flavouring that is particularly popular with young chefs. (Traditionalists, do not panic – the classic recipe is also given.) Although the custard for Crème Brûlée can be cooked and chilled a day before, it is important not to caramelize the topping until just before serving because it softens when left to stand too long. (The same is true of the caramel topping on Floating Islands on page 212 – melt and add the caramel just before serving.) Crème Brûlée is a staple of bistro menus, as is Crème Caramel (see page 209). Both desserts are made with the same basic ingredients – eggs, milk and sugar – and have a caramel top, but the results are quite different. Crème Caramel is slowly baked in a *bain marie* and when it is inverted onto a serving platter, the caramel becomes a sweet, golden-brown sauce. This is an ideal dessert for entertaining, as it is best made a day or two in advance and left to chill in the refrigerator until time to serve.

The ultimate French bistro dessert, however, has to be Chocolate Mousse (see page 216). One taste of this recipe and you will instantly be transported to a cosy French bistro, perhaps in Paris. It is creamy and irresistible and, again, it is good for entertaining as it can be made a day in advance and there aren't any last-minute preparations needed. Just be sure to use a good-quality chocolate with at least 70% cocoa butter for the richest flavour.

Bistro-style desserts are ideal for casual and everyday meals, but desserts that take a little more time and effort seem more suitable for dinner parties. Straight-from-the-oven Grand Marnier Soufflé (see page 215) has a retro style, but it provides a memorable end to any type of meal. Another retro

Vineyards are defining features of the French landscape: many sell their wares direct to the public

206

dessert that never loses its appeal is Crêpes Suzette (see page 219) with its delicious flambéed buttery orange-liqueur sauce.

Tarts, with their crisp, butter-rich pastry, are served in French bistros, restaurants and homes. Two of the most popular are creamy, zingy Lemon Tart (see page 225) and dark Chocolate Tartlets (see page 226). The sharp, fresh flavour of crème fraîche served with either of these contrasts well with the rich fillings. A traditional Apple Tart (see page 228) from Normandy, with the concentric rings of glazed apple slices on top, is easier than it looks to prepare. And the apple purée filling makes it less rich than custard-based tarts, so it can be served to end a substantial meal.

French farmers provide cooks with a vast array of flavoursome fruits, many of which are incorporated into desserts. Spiced Apricots in Red Wine (see page 231), with a hint of spice, and Peaches with Raspberry Sauce (see page 232) can well be made with fresh produce from the fertile Rhône or Loire valleys.

The irony of the French dessert course is that, even with so many mouthwatering creations to choose from, most everyday meals end with a piece of fruit and cheese. But, if both a cheese course and dessert course are served, the sweet will come after the cheese. 'Otherwise it is too much of a shock for the stomach to go from a savoury main course to the sweet dessert', as one Parisian gourmet noted. Others say serving the cheese course first is a logical way to finish any wine from the main meal. The French almost always drink coffee after dessert. Most typical is a small black espresso, but there are other options. A plain espresso is simply called a *café noir* or *express*. For espresso with a splash of milk, ask for *une noisette*, and for anyone trying to cut back on their caffeine intake, '*déca*' is the French shorthand for decaffeinated.

No market square in any town in France is complete without a game of boules in progress

crème caramel
crème caramel

Also called crème reversée, *this baked custard with its sweet golden caramel topping is popular with French domestic cooks as well as restaurateurs. This shouldn't be surprising, however, as once this is assembled, it can be left in the refrigerator and forgotten about for up to two days. It tastes best, in fact, if made a day in advance.*

SERVES 4–6

600 ml/1 pint full-fat milk

1 vanilla pod, split

175 g/6 oz caster sugar

4 tbsp water

squeeze of lemon juice

2 large eggs

2 large egg yolks

1 Preheat the oven to 160°C/325°F/Gas Mark 3. Lightly grease the sides of a 1.2-litre/2-pint soufflé dish.

2 Pour the milk into a small heavy-based saucepan. Use the tip of a knife to scrape the tiny seeds of the vanilla pod into the milk, then add the vanilla pod. Slowly bring the milk to the boil, then remove the pan from the heat and stir in 85 g/3 oz of the sugar, stirring until it dissolves. Leave to stand for at least 15 minutes to let the vanilla infuse.

3 Place the remaining sugar in another small heavy-based saucepan with the water over a medium heat. Stir until the sugar dissolves, then increase the heat and bring to the boil, without stirring. Continue boiling until the caramel turns a deep golden brown. Watch carefully as it can burn quickly.

4 Immediately squeeze a few drops of lemon juice into the caramel to stop the cooking. Pour the caramel into the prepared soufflé dish and swirl around, so that it coats the base.*

5 Bring a kettle of water to the boil. Beat the eggs and egg yolks together. Reheat the milk just until small bubbles appear around the sides, without boiling. Slowly pour the milk into the eggs, whisking constantly.

6 Strain the milk mixture through a fine sieve directly into the prepared soufflé dish and remove the vanilla pod. Transfer the soufflé dish to a roasting tin and pour in enough water to come halfway up the side of the dish.

7 Put the roasting tin in the oven and bake for 75–90 minutes until a knife inserted into the centre of the custard comes out clean. Remove the soufflé dish from the water and leave to cool completely. Cover with clingfilm and leave to chill for at least 24 hours.

8 To serve, run a round-bladed knife around the edge. Invert the Crème Caramel onto a serving dish with a rim, giving a good shake halfway over, then lift off the soufflé dish.

*cook's tip

If the caramel sets too quickly in Step 4, dip the base of the bowl in hot water until the caramel melts, then swirl it around again.

210

espresso crème brûlée
crème brûlée espresso

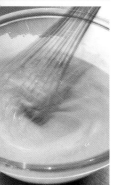

One of the great joys of French dining is to shatter the thin caramel topping on this ever-popular dessert to reveal the creamy custard filling underneath. Instant espresso powder gives a modern flavour to this version, but for a more traditional vanilla-flavoured dessert, see the variation below.

MAKES 4

450 ml/16 fl oz double cream

1 tbsp instant espresso powder

4 large egg yolks

100 g/3¹/₂ oz caster sugar

2 tbsp coffee liqueur, such as Kahlùa

4 tbsp caster sugar, for glazing

1 Preheat the oven to 110°C/225°F/Gas Mark ¹/₄ and put 4 shallow white porcelain dishes on a baking tray.

2 Place the cream in a small saucepan over a medium-high heat and heat just until small bubbles appear around the edges. Mix in the espresso powder, stirring until it dissolves, then remove the saucepan from the heat and leave until completely cool.

3 Lightly beat the egg yolks in a bowl, then add the sugar and continue beating until thick and creamy.

4 Reheat the cream over a medium-high heat until small bubbles appear around the edges. Stir the hot cream into the egg-yolk mixture, beating constantly. Stir in the coffee liqueur.

5 Divide the custard mixture between the dishes and bake the custards for 35–40 minutes, or until the custard is just 'trembling' when you shake the dishes.

6 Remove the lightly set custards from the oven and leave to cool completely. Cover the surfaces with clingfilm and leave to chill in the refrigerator for at least 4 hours, but ideally overnight.

7 Just before you are ready to serve, sprinkle the surface of each custard with the remaining sugar and caramelize with a kitchen blow-torch or put the dishes under a very hot preheated grill until the topping is golden and bubbling. Leave to cool for a few minutes for the caramel to harden before serving.

variation

For a traditional vanilla-flavoured crème brûlée, omit the espresso powder and Kahlùa. Add a slit vanilla pod to the hot cream in Step 4 and set aside to infuse for 1 hour. Use the tip of a small knife to scrape the tiny vanilla seeds into the cream, then reheat the cream and continue with the recipe.

Many French churches and public buildings are imaginatively lit at night, often to dramatic effect

212

floating islands
îles flottantes

This creamy dessert gets its name from the light, fluffy poached meringues that appear to be 'floating' in 'lakes' of vanilla-flavoured custard. 'Waste not, want not' is one of the mantras of traditional French domestic and professional kitchens, and the milk used to poach the meringues is then used to make the custard in this recipe.

SERVES 4–6

1 litre/1³/₄ pints milk, plus extra for the custard

1 vanilla pod, split

150 g/5¹/₂ oz caster sugar

6 egg yolks

1¹/₂ tbsp water

squeeze of lemon juice

for the meringues

2 large egg whites

¹/₄ tsp cream of tartar

55 g/2 oz caster sugar

55 g/2 oz icing sugar

1 Slowly bring the milk to the boil in a wide sauté or frying pan over a medium-high heat, then reduce the heat so small bubbles just lightly break the surface.

2 Meanwhile, to make the meringues, place the egg whites in a spotlessly clean bowl and beat using an electric mixer on low speed until broken up and frothy. Beat in the cream of tartar and continue beating until soft peaks form. At this point, gradually increase the mixer's speed and add the caster sugar, tablespoon by tablespoon, until stiff peaks form. Sift over the icing sugar and beat until the meringue is glossy and stiff.

3 Using a large tablespoon dipped in water, scoop up one-quarter of the meringue mixture and drop it into the simmering milk. Add 2 or 3 more meringues, but do not overcrowd the pan. Poach the meringues for 5 minutes. Use a slotted spoon to transfer the meringues to a folded tea towel and leave to drain. The meringues will deflate a little, but do not worry. Continue poaching meringues, if necessary, to make 4 in total.

4 Use a slotted spoon to remove any loose bits of meringue from the poaching milk, then strain it through a fine sieve. Re-measure the milk and make it up to 600 ml/1 pint with extra milk.

5 Place the milk in a heavy-based saucepan over a medium-high heat. Add the vanilla pod and slowly bring to the boil, then remove from the heat, cover the pan and leave to infuse for a few minutes.

6 Beat 100 g/3¹/₂ oz of the sugar in a bowl with the egg yolks until thick and creamy. Remove the vanilla pod from the milk, then pour one-quarter of the warm milk into the egg mixture, beating constantly.

7 Pour this mixture into the milk remaining in the saucepan, then return to the heat and simmer, stirring constantly, for 10 minutes, or until the custard thickens and coats the back of a spoon. Remove the custard from the heat and leave to cool completely, stirring occasionally.

8 Pour the custard into 4 bowls. Add the meringues, cover with clingfilm and leave to chill in the refrigerator for at least 2 hours or for up to 24.

9 To finish the dish, just before serving make the caramel. Place the remaining sugar in a small heavy-based saucepan over a medium-high heat with

the water. Stir to dissolve the sugar, then bring to the boil, without stirring. Leave the mixture to bubble until it turns a dark golden brown, then immediately remove the saucepan from the heat and add the lemon juice to stop the cooking.

10 Remove the custard and meringues from the refrigerator and uncover. Use a teaspoon to drizzle the caramel back and forth over the surface of the custard and meringues. It will harden immediately it hits the cold surface.

A classic French ending to any meal. A soufflé is not difficult to make, but it does require the cook to be ready to act quickly as soon as it comes out of the oven or it will deflate before it arrives at the table. To guarantee 'oohs and aahs', have a plate ready on which to put the hot soufflé dish and icing sugar in a sieve ready to sift over the top, then quickly take the soufflé to the table. A perfectly cooked soufflé will have a thin crust on top with a soft centre.

grand marnier soufflé   215
soufflé au grand marnier

SERVES 4

butter, for greasing

55 g/2 oz caster sugar, plus a little extra for the dish

3 large eggs, separated, plus 1 large egg
  and 1 large egg white

4 tbsp plain flour

300 ml/10 fl oz full-fat milk

¹/₄ tsp vanilla extract

¹/₂ tbsp finely grated orange rind

2¹/₂ tbsp Grand Marnier

¹/₄ tsp cream of tartar

icing sugar, to decorate

1 Preheat the oven to 180°C/350°F/Gas Mark 4 with a baking tray inside, positioned in the bottom third of the oven. Grease the sides of a 1.7-litre/3-pint soufflé dish with butter and sprinkle with a little caster sugar, then tip out the excess.

2 Using an electric mixer, beat the caster sugar, 1 whole egg and 1 egg yolk together until blended and a pale yellow colour, scraping down the sides of the bowl as necessary.

3 Stir in the flour, then slowly beat in the milk and vanilla extract. Transfer the mixture to a heavy-based saucepan over a medium-high heat and slowly bring to the boil, beating constantly, until a smooth, thick custard forms. Reduce the heat to low and simmer, still beating, for 2 minutes.

4 Remove the pan from the heat and beat in the remaining egg yolks, one by one, then leave to stand to allow the *crème pâtissière* to cool slightly. Beat in the orange rind and Grand Marnier.

5 Meanwhile, wash and completely dry the mixer's beaters. Place all the egg whites in a spotlessly clean bowl and beat on a low speed until they are broken up and frothy. Beat in the cream of tartar and continue whisking the egg whites until soft peaks form. At this point, gradually increase the mixer's speed and continue beating until stiff peaks form.

6 Beat several tablespoons of the egg whites into the custard to loosen. Transfer the custard mixture to the bowl with the egg whites and use a large metal spoon or rubber spatula to lightly but quickly fold the mixtures together with a figure-of-eight motion.

7 Spoon the soufflé mixture into the prepared soufflé dish, which will only be about three-quarters full. Put the dish on the hot baking tray and bake for 45 minutes until well risen and golden on top. Dust the top with icing sugar and serve at once.*

*cook's tip
A puffy, well-risen soufflé always makes an impressive dinner party dessert, but it does require planning ahead as the egg whites have to be whisked at the last minute before the dish goes in the oven. Steps 1–4 can be done ahead of time, ready for the egg whites to be whisked after the main course. Then, while the soufflé is baking, continue the meal French style and serve a cheese course before dessert.

216

chocolate mousse
mousse au chocolat

For the perfect do-ahead dessert for a bistro-style meal, this rich mousse will not disappoint.

SERVES 4–6

225 g/8 oz plain chocolate, chopped

2 tbsp brandy, Grand Marnier or Cointreau

4 tbsp water

30 g/1 oz unsalted butter, diced

3 large eggs, separated

¼ tsp cream of tartar

55 g/2 oz sugar

125 ml/4 fl oz double cream

1 Place the chocolate, brandy and water in a small saucepan over a low heat and melt, stirring, until smooth. Remove the saucepan from the heat and beat in the butter.

2 Beat the egg yolks into the chocolate mixture, one after another, until blended, then leave to cool slightly.

3 Meanwhile, using an electric mixer on low speed, beat the egg whites in a spotlessly clean bowl until they are frothy, then gradually increase the mixer's speed and beat until soft peaks form. Sprinkle the cream of tartar over the surface, then add the sugar, tablespoon by tablespoon, and continue beating until stiff peaks form. Beat several tablespoons of the egg whites into the chocolate mixture to loosen.

4 In another bowl, whip the cream until soft peaks form. Spoon the cream over the chocolate mixture, then spoon the remaining whites over the cream. Use a large metal spoon or rubber spatula to fold the chocolate into the cream and egg whites.

5 Either spoon the chocolate mousse into a large serving bowl or divide it between 4 or 6 individual bowls. Cover the bowl(s) with clingfilm and chill the mousse for at least 3 hours before serving.

The snow-covered mountains of the Alps and the Massif Central are only a short step away from the balmy Riviera

crêpes suzette
crêpes suzette

This dessert is probably what comes to mind when anyone thinks of flambéing in fancy French restaurants, with a waiter preparing and lighting the sauce at the side of the table. Some food historians say Crêpes Suzette *were accidentally created when a sauce for crepes ordered by the Prince of Wales, later Kind Edward VII, caught fire in the dining room at the Café Royale in Monte Carlo, while others say the dish was created in honour of an actress named Suzanne 'Suzette' Reichenberg. In either case, this classic dessert is easy to prepare at home. To make fresh Crêpes turn to page 247.*

SERVES 4

**8 Sweet Crêpes made with the finely grated rind
  of 1 lemon added to the batter**

2 tbsp brandy

for the Orange Sauce

55 g/2 oz caster sugar

1 tbsp water

finely grated rind of 1 large orange

125 ml/4 fl oz freshly squeezed orange juice

55 g/2 oz unsalted butter, diced

**1 tbsp Cointreau, Grand Marnier or other orange-
  flavoured liqueur**

1 To make the Orange Sauce, place the sugar in a wide sauté or frying pan over a medium heat and stir in the water. Continue stirring until the sugar dissolves, then increase the heat to high and leave the syrup to bubble for 1–2 minutes until it just begins to turn golden brown.

2 Stir in the orange rind and juice, then add the butter and continue stirring until it melts. Stir in the orange-flavoured liqueur.

3 Lay one of the crêpes flat in the sauté pan and spoon the sauce over. Using a fork and the spoon, fold the crêpe into quarters and push to the side of the pan. Add the next crêpe to the pan and repeat. Continue until all the crêpes are coated with the sauce and folded. Remove the pan from the heat.

4 Warm the brandy in a ladle or small saucepan, ignite and pour it over the crêpes to flambé, shaking the sauté pan.

5 When the flames die down, serve the crêpes with the sauce spooned over.

Overleaf The pâtisserie and its tempting display of mouth-watering delights is a familiar sight anywhere in France

222

poached pears with chocolate sauce
poires belle hélène

Poires belle-hélène *is a classic French dessert that involves poaching whole pears in a sugar syrup. This is a quicker, easier home-style dessert, like a hot-fudge sundae for adults.*

SERVES 4

4 ripe pears, such as Conference

juice of ¹/₂ lemon

350 ml/12 fl oz Beaumes-de-Venise dessert wine

175 ml/6 fl oz water

1 vanilla pod, split*

vanilla ice cream, to serve

for the Chocolate Sauce

175 g/6 oz plain chocolate, chopped

75 ml/2¹/₂ fl oz water

4 tbsp double cream

1 To prepare the pears, peel, core and quarter, dropping each quarter into a bowl of water with the lemon juice squeezed in to prevent it from turning brown while the others are prepared.

2 Put the wine, water and split vanilla pod in a sauté or frying pan over a high heat. Add the pear quarters and bring the liquid to the boil. As soon as it boils, reduce the heat just until small bubbles appear around the edge.

3 Poach the pears until they are tender when pierced with the tip of a knife. The exact poaching time will depend on how ripe the pears are – some will be tender within 5 minutes, while others can take 12–15 minutes.

4 Use a slotted spoon to transfer the pear quarters to an ovenproof serving dish as they become tender. When all the pears are removed from the liquid, return the liquid to the boil and boil until reduced to about 4 tablespoons.

5 Pour the syrup and vanilla pod over the pears and leave to cool completely. Cover the surface with clingfilm and chill for at least 1 hour or overnight.

6 Just before serving, make the Chocolate Sauce. Put the chocolate and water in a small saucepan over a low heat and melt, stirring, until smooth. Remove the saucepan from the heat and beat in the cream.

7 Spoon a scoop of ice cream into individual serving bowls and add the poached pears. Spoon over the hot Chocolate Sauce and serve at once.

*cook's tip

Vanilla pods are expensive, but they can be used more than once. Remove the pod from the cool syrup, then rinse, pat dry with kitchen paper and use to make Vanilla Sugar.

lemon tart
tarte au citron

One bite of this elegantly simple tart will instantly transport you to France – the creamy citrus filling providing a perfect contrast to the crisp, buttery pastry. It's no wonder Lemon Tart features on dessert menus everywhere in the country.

SERVES 8

1 quantity Sweet Tart Pastry

finely grated rind of 3 lemons

150 ml/5 fl oz freshly squeezed lemon juice
 from 3 or 4 large lemons

100 g/3^1/$_2$ oz caster sugar

150 ml/5 fl oz crème fraîche

3 large eggs

3 large egg yolks

icing sugar, to dust

1 To partially bake the pastry case blind, preheat the oven to 200°C/400°F/Gas Mark 6 with a baking tray inside. Prepare the pastry, roll it out and use to line a 23-cm/9-inch fluted tart tin with a removable base, leaving the excess pastry hanging over the edge. Line the pastry case with a larger piece of greaseproof paper, then fill with ceramic baking beans, dried beans or rice.

2 Put the lined tart tin on the baking tray and bake for 10–15 minutes until the pastry rim looks set. Remove the paper and beans or rice and return the pastry case to the oven for a further 5 minutes, or until the base looks dry. Remove the pastry case from the oven, leave it on the baking tray and reduce the oven temperature to 190°C/375°F/Gas Mark 5.

3 Meanwhile, beat the lemon rind, lemon juice and caster sugar together until the sugar dissolves. Slowly beat in the crème fraîche until blended, then beat in the eggs and yolks, 1 at a time.

4 Carefully pour the filling into the pastry case, then transfer to the oven and bake for 20–30 minutes until the filling is set and the pastry is golden brown. If the pastry or the filling look as though they are becoming too brown, cover the tart with a sheet of foil.

5 Transfer the tart to a wire rack to cool completely before rolling a rolling pin over the edge to remove the excess pastry. To serve, remove the tin, transfer to a serving platter and dust with icing sugar.

variation

This creamy filling includes the grated lemon rind. For a perfectly smooth tart, however, leave the filling to stand for at least 30 minutes, then strain it into the pastry case.

The café in the market square forms the social centre of the typical French village

226

chocolate tartlets
tartelettes au chocolat

Rich, dark chocolate, in one guise or another, often provides a satisfying end to French meals and these tartlets are no exception. The sharp flavour of crème fraîche sets off the intense chocolate flavour of the filling.

MAKES 4

1 quantity Sweet Tart Pastry

150 g/5¹/₂ oz plain chocolate, broken into pieces

50 g/1³/₄ oz butter

100 ml/3¹/₂ fl oz whipping cream

1 large egg

30 g/1 oz caster sugar

cocoa powder, to decorate

crème fraîche, to serve

1 To partially bake the pastry cases blind, preheat the oven to 200°C/400°F/Gas Mark 6 with a baking tray inside. Prepare the pastry, roll it out and use to line 4 x 12-cm/4¹/₂-inch fluted tart tins with removable bases as instructed on page 250, leaving the excess pastry hanging over the edges. Line the pastry cases with larger pieces of greaseproof paper, then fill with ceramic baking beans, dried beans or rice.

2 Put the lined tart tins on the baking tray and bake for 5 minutes, or until the pastry rims look set. Remove the paper and beans or rice and return the pastry cases to the oven for a further 5 minutes, or until the bases look dry. Remove the pastry cases from the oven, leave them on the baking tray and reduce the oven temperature to 180°C/350°F/Gas Mark 4.

3 Meanwhile, place the chocolate in a heatproof bowl set over a saucepan of simmering water so that the bowl does not touch the water. Add the butter and cream and leave until the chocolate and butter melt.

4 Beat the egg and sugar together until light and fluffy. Remove the melted chocolate mixture from the heat and stir until smooth, then stir it into the egg mixture.

5 Carefully pour the filling into the tart cases, then transfer to the oven and bake for 15 minutes, or until the filling is set and the pastry is golden brown. If the pastry looks as though it is becoming too brown, cover it with a sheet of foil.

6 Transfer the tartlets to a wire rack to cool completely before rolling a rolling pin over the edges to remove the excess pastry. To serve, remove from the tins, transfer to individual plates and dust with cocoa powder. Put a dollop of crème fraîche on the side of each plate.

variations

To make a 23-cm/9-inch tart, prepare 1 quantity Sweet Tart Pastry, then roll out, line the tin and partially bake blind as for the Lemon Tart. Use the quantities for the filling as above, but increase the baking time in Step 5 to 20 minutes.

These tartlets look attractive with small chocolate curls arranged in the centre of each. Chill a bar of plain chocolate, then run a vegetable peeler from top to bottom along a thin edge. Use a cocktail stick to transfer the curls to the top of the tartlets.

228

apple tart
tarte aux pommes

French pâtisserie windows display a tempting range of sweet and savoury tarts, often including glistening apple tarts with concentric rings of apple slices on top. It is surprisingly easy to make this popular dessert at home. This tart, from Normandy, has an apple purée filling, which makes a lighter tart than those filled with crème pâtissière *and poached apples.*

SERVES 8

8 large, firm apples, about 1 kg/2 lb 4 oz, such as
  Granny Smiths or Cox's

100 g/3^1/$_2$ oz Vanilla Sugar

2 tbsp water

1 quantity Sweet Tart Pastry

1 egg white, lightly beaten

2 tbsp apricot jam

1 Reserve 4 apples, then peel, halve, core and chop the remainder. Put the chopped apples in a heavy-based saucepan over a medium-high heat and stir in the sugar and water. Stir the apples constantly for 20 minutes, or until they break down and form a thick purée and the excess liquid has evaporated. Leave to cool completely.

2 Meanwhile, to partially bake the pastry case blind, preheat the oven to 200°C/400°F/Gas Mark 6 with a baking tray inside. Prepare the pastry, roll it out and use to line a 23-cm/9-inch fluted tart tin with a removable base, leaving the excess pastry hanging over the edge. Line the pastry case with a larger piece of greaseproof paper, then fill with ceramic baking beans, dried beans or rice.

3 Place the lined tart tin on the baking tray and bake for 10-15 minutes, or until the pastry rim looks set. Remove the paper and beans or rice and brush the base with the egg white. Return the pastry case to the oven for a further 5 minutes, or until the base looks dry. Remove the pastry case from the oven and leave it on the baking tray. Do not turn off the oven.

4 Peel, quarter and core the remaining apples, then cut them into very thin slices. Spread the apple purée over the base of the pastry case. Arrange the apple slices in overlapping concentric circles to cover the entire surface, starting on the outer edge and working towards the centre.

5 Return the tart to the oven and bake for 35–40 minutes, or until the pastry is crisp and golden brown. If the pastry looks as though it is becoming too brown, cover it with strips of foil.

6 Meanwhile, place the jam in a small saucepan over a medium heat until it melts and forms a thick syrup. As soon as the tart comes out of the oven, brush the surface with the jam, then transfer the tart to a wire rack to cool completely before rolling a rolling pin over the edge to remove the excess pastry. To serve, remove the tin and transfer to a serving platter.

spiced apricots in red wine

abricots au vin rouge quatre-épices

The Rhône Valley is one of France's main apricot-growing centres, so a full-bodied red wine from the region is a natural choice for this lightly spiced dessert. Try one from the ancient commune of Châteauneuf-du-Pape or one labelled as Hermitage, made from grapes grown on the side of the hill of the same name.

SERVES 4–6

¹/₂ tsp white peppercorns, lightly crushed

3 cloves

350 ml/12 fl oz full-bodied red wine,
   such as Côtes du Rhône

200 ml/7 fl oz water

200 g/7 oz sugar

1-cm/¹/₂-inch piece of fresh root ginger, peeled
   and finely sliced

1 cinnamon stick

6 tender fresh apricots

freshly grated nutmeg

2 tbsp toasted flaked almonds, to decorate

crème fraîche, to serve (optional)

1 Place the peppercorns and cloves in a dry sauté or frying pan over a high heat and toast, stirring constantly, for 1 minute, or until the aroma develops. Immediately tip them out of the pan. Place the peppercorns in a mortar and lightly crush with a pestle .

2 Put the wine, water, sugar, peppercorns, cloves, ginger and cinnamon stick in a heavy-based saucepan over a high heat and stir to dissolve the sugar.* When the sugar has dissolved, bring the liquid to the boil, without stirring, and leave to boil for 8 minutes.

3 Add the apricots to the syrup, reduce the heat to low and simmer for 5 minutes, or until just tender when pierced with the tip of a knife. Use a slotted spoon to remove the apricots from the syrup and transfer to a bowl of iced water to cool.

4 When the apricots are cool enough to handle, peel them, then cut them in half, remove the stones and transfer to a serving bowl.

5 Meanwhile, return the syrup to the boil and boil until it becomes thick. Grate in the nutmeg to taste. Remove the syrup from the heat and leave it to cool, then pour it over the apricot halves. Cover and chill the apricots until required.

6 Serve the apricots with a generous portion of the syrup, the toasted flaked almonds and a dollop of crème fraîche on the side, if you like.

*cook's tip

The spices look attractive left in the syrup for serving. If you prefer a plain sauce, however, tie the peppercorns, cloves, ginger and cinnamon stick in a piece of muslin before adding them to the wine for easy removal.

peaches with raspberry sauce
pêches à la cardinale

The bright pink-red colour of the sauce gives this summer dish its French name, referring to its similarity to the vibrant colour of cardinals' robes.

SERVES 4-6

450 g/1 lb fresh raspberries*

finely grated rind of 1 orange

2 tbsp freshly squeezed orange juice

2 tbsp Grand Marnier, Cointreau or other orange-
   flavoured liqueur

2-3 tbsp caster sugar

6 ripe fresh peaches

to serve

vanilla ice cream

langues de chat biscuits (optional)

1 Purée the raspberries in a food processor or blender, then press through a fine non-metallic sieve into a mixing bowl to remove the seeds.

2 Stir the orange rind and juice and liqueur into the raspberry purée. Add sugar to taste, stirring until the sugar dissolves. Cover and leave to chill in the refrigerator until required.

3 Meanwhile, bring a large saucepan of water to the boil over a high heat. Add the peaches, 1 or 2 at a time, and leave for 10–20 seconds, then remove with a slotted spoon. When the peaches are cool enough to handle, peel off the skins, then cut them in half and remove the stones.

4 Cut each peach half into quarters and stir into the raspberry sauce. Cover and leave to chill in the refrigerator until required.

5 When ready to serve, put a scoop or two of ice cream into individual glasses or bowls, then top with the peaches and spoon some extra sauce over. Serve with the biscuits on the side, if you like.

*cook's tip
When fresh raspberries are not in season, use frozen ones.

cherry clafoutis
clafoutis aux cerises

This baked batter dessert with black cherries from Limousin was devised as a way to use up over-ripe fruit. The traditional recipe is made with small unstoned cherries as it was thought that if the skins were broken too much flavour would be lost.

SERVES 6

450 g/1 lb ripe fresh cherries, stoned

100 g/3¹/₂ oz caster sugar

2 large eggs

1 egg yolk

100 g/3¹/₂ oz plain flour

pinch of salt

175 ml/6 fl oz full-fat milk

4 tbsp double cream

1 tsp vanilla extract or almond essence

1 Preheat the oven to 200°C/400°F/Gas Mark 6. Lightly grease a 1.2-litre/2-pint ovenproof serving dish or a 25-cm/10-inch quiche dish. Scatter the cherries over the base of the prepared dish, then place the dish on a baking tray.

2 Using an electric mixer, whisk the sugar, eggs and the egg yolk together until blended and a pale yellow colour, scraping down the sides of the bowl as necessary.

3 Beat in the flour and salt, then slowly beat in the milk, cream and vanilla extract until a light, smooth batter forms. Pour the batter into the dish.

4 Transfer the filled dish on the baking tray to the oven and bake for 45 minutes, or until the top is golden brown and the batter is set.

5 Leave the pudding to stand for at least 5 minutes, then serve hot, lukewarm or at room temperature.

variation

When fresh cherries are out of season, substitute 425 g/15 oz canned stoned cherries in syrup. Rinse the cherries well, then pat dry before putting them in the dish.

SAUCES & BASICS

236 This chapter focuses on the basic recipes that give authentic French flavours to everyday meals. French cooking is not difficult, but it is worth mastering the recipes that cooks use on a daily basis when attempting to recreate the French style at home. In many cases, these basic recipes have been handed down from generation to generation. A busy modern-day Parisian cook making pastry, salad dressing or mayonnaise in preparation for a family meal or dinner party will be doing exactly what his or her grandmother would have done in the same situation.

For anyone who has only ever tasted commercial varieties, the subtle flavour of home-made Mayonnaise (see page 241) will be a revelation. But an even greater revelation will be how easy it is to make. It is virtually foolproof as long as the ingredients are at room temperature when you begin, and the oil is slowly added, drop by drop, until an emulsion forms and the mixture begins to thicken. And after mastering the basic mayonnaise recipe, it is only a matter of adaptation to make a variety of other French sauces: Aïoli (known as 'the butter of Provence'), Tartare Sauce (perfect with fried fish), and chilli-flavoured *rouille* (essential with bouillabaisse).

Wherever you go in France, mixed-leaf salads are lightly dressed with Vinaigrette (see page 244), a simple emulsion formed by whisking oil (*huile*) with vinegar (*vinaigre*). Vinaigrette-making is often a job for the man of the house, even if all other kitchen chores are left to someone else. However, making an authentic French-tasting vinaigrette couldn't be easier and for creative cooks the scope for variations is unlimited, depending on the type of oil and flavour of vinegar or mustard used. French supermarkets stock many brands of prepared vinaigrettes, but many home cooks keep a selection of high-quality oils, vinegars and mustards in their cupboards to make a vinaigrette for each meal. French oils and vinegars make excellent inexpensive souvenirs from trips to France, and the choice in supermarkets is large.

French pastry-making can be elevated to a high art form. In France, the pastry shops (*pâtisseries*) have tempting window displays of freshly baked sweet tarts with beautifully arranged fresh fruit, shiny glazes, dark chocolate and creamy fillings, all in golden pastry cases. When the display tempts you through the threshold into the shop, you are greeted by the delectable smell of butter. That is because, unlike British and American cooks who often include lard

Previous page '*Formidable' applies as much to the cuisine of Paris as to the shows of the Moulin Rouge*

The Grande Arche de la Défense in Paris assumes pride of place among the splendid monuments of the city

or vegetable fats in their pastry dough for a flaky result, French pastry chefs only use butter. The result is crisp, rich, melt-in-the-mouth pastry. The need for crisper pastry is evident with a closer look at the window displays: French tarts are presented unmoulded and free-standing. If you've ever wondered how so many pastry shops can thrive, it is because most home cooks prefer to buy a baked tart rather than to make one. The high butter content of French pastry also makes the dough difficult to work with. If you want to make your own French pastry, however, Savoury Tart Pastry (see page 249) and Sweet Tart Pastry (see page 250) will capture the unmistakable flavours of tarts from a French pâtisserie.

The importance of home-made Chicken, Vegetable and Fish Stocks (see pages 252–3) in French cooking is evident in the French word '*fond*', which means 'foundation'. These flavoured liquids, made with chicken and fish bones and vegetable trimmings along with other flavourings, give the 'backbone' to soups, stews, casseroles and sauces, all essential to cooking *à la française*. One of the bonuses of home-made stocks is their versatility and stock-making does not have to be a chore. When time is short, for example, freeze the bones left over after a meal until there is time to make a large potful. Then leave the stock to cool and freeze it in convenient-sized portions, ready to use when required.

Another excellent freezer standby is Crêpes (see page 247). Easy to make, they thaw quickly to make savoury snacks, or one of the most classic of all French desserts, Crêpes Suzette (see page 219). And for one of the quickest desserts, just reheat a crêpe in a pan, then spread with butter and sprinkle with sugar.

mayonnaise
sauce mayonnaise

One of the basic sauces in the French culinary repertoire, home-made mayonnaise has a milder flavour than most commercial varieties.

MAKES ABOUT 300 ML/10 FL OZ

2 large egg yolks
2 tsp Dijon mustard
³/₄ tsp salt, or to taste
2 tbsp lemon juice or white wine vinegar
about 300 ml/10 fl oz sunflower oil
white pepper

1 Whiz the egg yolks with the Dijon mustard, salt and white pepper to taste in a food processor, blender or by hand. Add the lemon juice and whiz again.

2 With the motor still running or still beating, add the oil, drop by drop at first. When the sauce begins to thicken, the oil can then be added in a slow, steady stream. Taste and adjust the seasoning with extra salt, pepper and lemon juice if necessary. If the sauce seems too thick, slowly add 1 tablespoon hot water, single cream or lemon juice.

3 Use at once or store in an airtight container in the refrigerator for up to 1 week.

variations
Aïoli (*Aïoli*) Add 4 crushed garlic cloves, or to taste, in Step 1 and whiz with the egg yolks, mustard and salt and pepper. Continue with the recipe as above.
Tartare Sauce (*Sauce Tartare*) Stir in 10 finely chopped cornichons, 1 tablespoon finely chopped rinsed and dried capers and 1 tablespoon very finely chopped fresh flat-leaf parsley.

Beautiful medieval chateaux and walled cities dot the landscape in the mountainous regions of France

242

onion marmalade
marmelade d'oignons

A pot of this slowly cooked, sweet onion mixture is handy to have in the refrigerator. It's a natural partner for Chicken Liver Pâté or Country-style Terrine and perks up simple chops or steaks. It also goes well with blue cheeses such as Roquefort.

MAKES ABOUT 750 G/1 LB 10 OZ

40 g/1½ oz unsalted butter

1 tbsp sunflower oil

900 g/2 lb onions, thinly sliced

100 g/3½ oz soft light brown sugar

3 tbsp red wine vinegar

1½ tbsp crème de cassis

1½ tsp salt, to taste

1 Melt the butter with the oil in a large sauté or frying pan or a heavy-based saucepan over a medium-high heat.* Add the onions and stir them around for 5 minutes.

2 Stir in the sugar, vinegar, cassis and salt, stirring until the sugar dissolves. Reduce the heat to its lowest setting and leave the onions to cook, stirring occasionally, for 1¼-1½ hours until they are very soft and dark brown. Watch carefully towards the end so that they don't burn because that will make them taste bitter.

3 Remove from the heat and leave to cool completely. Store in an airtight container in the refrigerator for up to 2 weeks.

cook's tip
Use the widest pan available as it will speed up the cooking time.

France boasts some of the world's most ancient, stunning and captivating cathedrals

244
vinaigrette
vinaigrette

The French have never developed a liking for thick, creamy salad dressings. Instead, this basic emulsion of oil and vinegar is used throughout the country, with occasional flavour variations, although on the whole the basic recipe is preferred. This dressing is a great way to capture the flavour of French salads, and with so few ingredients, it is essential to use good-quality oil and vinegar. Olive and other vegetable oils give a different character to the dressing. In the South of France, olive oil is always used, while in other parts of the country, chefs occasionally reach for sunflower or groundnut oil.

MAKES ABOUT 150 ML/5 FL OZ

125 ml/4 fl oz olive or other vegetable oil

3 tbsp white wine vinegar or lemon juice

1 tsp Dijon mustard

$\frac{1}{2}$ tsp caster sugar

salt and pepper

1 Using a stick blender, put all the ingredients in a jar, then blend until a thick emulsion forms. Alternatively, put all the ingredients in a screw-top jar, secure the lid and shake vigorously until the emulsion forms. Taste and adjust the seasoning if necessary.

2 Use at once or store in an airtight container in the refrigerator for up to a month. Always whisk or shake the dressing again before using.

variations

Garlic Vinaigrette (*Vinaigrette d'ail*) Use a good-quality garlic-flavoured oil and add 1 or 2 crushed garlic cloves to taste. The longer the garlic cloves are left in the dressing, the more pronounced the flavour will be, but they should be removed after a week.

Herb Vinaigrette (*Vinaigrette d'herbe*) Stir 1$\frac{1}{2}$ tablespoons chopped fresh herbs, such as chives, parsley or mint, or a mixture, into the above dressing. Use within 3 days and strain through a fine non-metallic sieve if the herbs begin to darken.

Walnut Vinaigrette (*Vinaigrette de noix*) Use a good-quality walnut oil and add 2 tablespoons chopped walnuts just before using.

Raspberry Vinaigrette (*Vinaigrette de framboise*) Replace the white wine vinegar with a good-quality raspberry-flavoured vinegar and add a few drops of fresh orange juice. Pour the vinegar over 85 g/3 oz crushed raspberries and leave to infuse for up to 3 hours at room temperature. Strain through a fine non-metallic sieve. If the vinegar tastes too tart, stir in a little extra sugar.

The wide, tree-lined boulevards of French cities are flanked by restaurants and bars for al fresco eating

crêpes 247
crêpes

Practice makes perfect – and after making crêpes once or twice, the technique can become second nature. And it is a technique worth mastering as crêpes have many uses for simple savoury meals and desserts. In Paris, vendors add various flavourings to hot-off-the-grill crêpes to make the French version of street food for eating while walking through the Tuileries Gardens or along the Seine. Capture the flavour of strolling through Paris in the spring by adding caster sugar with lemon juice to the just-cooked crêpes, then folding into quarters – ideal for eating on the go. Or melt a knob of butter over the hot surface, then top with Vanilla Sugar and a splash of Grand Marnier. For the easiest of ideas, spread with chocolate and hazelnut spread.

MAKES 9 (THE FIRST CRÊPE IS TRADITIONALLY A 'TEST' AND THE COOK'S TREAT)

115 g/4 oz plain flour

pinch of salt

1–2 tbsp caster sugar

2 large eggs

300 ml/10 fl oz milk

30 g/1 oz butter, melted and cooled

sunflower oil

1 Sift the flour, salt and 1 tablespoon of the sugar into a large bowl and make a deep well in the centre. If you are making sweet crêpes for a dessert, add an extra tablespoon of sugar.

2 Put the eggs and a little of the milk into the well and beat them together. Gradually draw in the flour from the sides as you beat. Stir in the butter, then gradually add the remaining milk until the batter has the consistency of single cream, stirring constantly to prevent lumps forming.

3 Cover the bowl and leave the batter to stand for at least 30 minutes. You can leave it in the refrigerator for up to 24 hours, but remember to remove the batter from the refrigerator at least 15 minutes before cooking.

4 When you are ready to cook, give the batter another good beating. Heat a 20-cm/8-inch crêpe pan or frying pan over a high heat, then very lightly wipe the surface with sunflower oil, using a crumpled piece of kitchen paper.

5 Turn down the heat under the pan to medium. Ladle 45 ml/1½ oz fl oz or 3 tablespoons of the batter into the middle of the pan and immediately swirl the batter around so it covers the base thinly.

6 Cook for 1 minute, or until the edge is golden and the batter is set and golden brown on the bottom. Use a metal spatula to flip the crêpe over and repeat on the other side.

7 Transfer the crêpe to a plate and continue to make 8 more crêpes, placing a piece of greaseproof paper between each one on the plate. The crêpes can then be stored in the refrigerator for up to 48 hours or frozen. Alternatively, they can be used immediately or kept warm wrapped in foil and placed on a plate over a saucepan of simmering water.

savoury tart pastry
pâte brisée

The French name for this crisp, butter-rich pastry translates as 'broken dough'. Unlike flakier and lighter British and American pastries, this French version is intended for free-standing tarts that are moved out of the tart tin after cooling. French bakers traditionally make their pastry with a large mound of flour on the work surface, but making it in a bowl produces the same result and is neater. A food processor can also be used, but much care has to be taken not to overprocess the pastry or it will be tough when it is baked.

MAKES A 23-CM/9-INCH TART OR 4 X 12-CM/4¹/₂-INCH TARTLETS

175 g/6 oz plain flour

¹/₂ tsp salt

75 g/3 oz chilled unsalted butter, diced

2-3 tbsp chilled water

1 Sift the flour and salt into a large bowl. Add the butter and use a pastry blender or 2 knives scissor-fashion to cut the butter into the flour until crumbs the size of peas form.

2 Sprinkle 2 tablespoons of the water over the surface and use a knife to mix it in. The pastry should start coming together at this point, but if it is dry and crumbly, lightly sprinkle with a little extra water.

3 Gather the pastry into a rough ball and turn it out onto a sheet of greaseproof paper. Shape it into a ball, handling as lightly as possible, then wrap up in the greaseproof paper and transfer to the refrigerator for at least 30 minutes, although it can be refrigerated for up to 24 hours at this point.

4 If the pastry is refrigerated for longer than 1 hour, leave it to stand for at least 10 minutes before rolling out.

5 To roll out the pastry, unwrap the dough and place it on a lightly floured work surface. Using a lightly floured rolling pin, roll the pastry into a 30-cm/12-inch round, rolling from the centre outwards and turning the pastry at 45-degree angles. Handle it as little as possible and roll it to an even thickness.

6 To line a 23-cm/9-inch tart tin, lift the dough over the rolling pin, then place it over the tart tin and unroll. Ease the pastry onto the base of the tin and up the sides.* Leave the excess pastry hanging over the edge to trim off after baking, just trimming it so that it will not touch the baking tray.

7 The pastry case is now ready to use at once, or it can be covered and chilled for up to 24 hours.

*cook's tip

To avoid overhandling the pastry when lining the tin in Step 6, mould a little of the excess pastry into a ball and use that, rather than your fingertips, to ease the pastry into the sides of the tin.

250

sweet tart pastry
pâte sucrée

The egg yolks in this pastry give it an extra-crisp texture that holds free-standing tarts with creamy fillings. The high butter content makes it very 'short', or difficult to work with. If it becomes too soft and sticky, put it in the refrigerator for 15 minutes before continuing to avoid overworking it, which will produce a tough texture.

**MAKES A 23-CM/9-INCH TART
OR 4 X 12-CM/4¹/₂-INCH TARTLETS**

150 g/5¹/₂ oz plain flour

¹/₂ tsp salt

3 tbsp caster sugar

2 large egg yolks beaten with 1 tsp chilled water

¹/₂ tsp vanilla extract (optional)

115 g/4 oz unsalted butter at room temperature, diced

1 Sift the flour and salt into a bowl and make a deep well in the centre.

2 Add the sugar, egg yolks and vanilla extract, if using, to the well and mix together with your fingertips. Add the butter and quickly work it into the other ingredients in the well.

3 Use a dough scraper or palette knife to draw the flour in from the sides of the bowl and continue working the butter and flour together with your fingertips until fine crumbs form. Very lightly use the heel of your hand to 'knead' the pastry until it is smooth and pliable. Shape the pastry into a ball, wrap it in greaseproof paper and chill for at least 30 minutes, although it can be refrigerated for up to 24 hours at this point.

4 If the pastry is refrigerated for longer than 1 hour, leave it to stand for at least 10 minutes before rolling out.

5 To roll out the pastry, unwrap the dough and place it on a lightly floured work surface. Using a lightly floured rolling pin, roll the pastry into a 30-cm/12-inch round, rolling from the centre outwards and turning the pastry at 45-degree angles. Handle it as little as possible and roll it to an even thickness.

6 To line a 23-cm/9-inch tart tin, lift the dough over the rolling pin, then place it over the tart tin and unroll. Use a small piece of the extra pastry shaped into a ball to ease the pastry onto the base of the tin and up the sides. Leave the excess pastry hanging over the edge to trim off after baking, just trimming it so that it will not touch the baking tray.

7 The pastry case is now ready to use at once, or it can be covered and chilled for up to 24 hours.*

*cook's tip
Tart cases made with sweet pastry, especially individual ones, are delicate and break easily. To avoid this, leave the baked cases to cool completely in the tart tins and fill them before unmoulding. Watch carefully as the pastry is being baked, as it can overbrown and scorch quickly. If the pastry appears to be overbaking, cover the edges with strips of foil squeezed to fit around the rim.

stocks
les fonds

The importance of good-quality stock in French cooking cannot be overemphasized – the French term for stock is 'fond de cuisine', or 'the foundation of cooking'. Stock is a clear liquid, made from simmering bones and flavourings, that transforms soups and sauces, stews and casseroles by adding extra flavour and body. Stock cubes are a quick alternative to making fresh stock, but the flavours are not as subtle. A better short cut is to use the fresh stocks sold in supermarkets, which have more of the flavours and body of home-made stocks.

chicken stock

MAKES ABOUT 1.2 LITRES/2 PINTS

1 roast chicken carcass, plus any extra bones*

1.7 litres/3 pints water

2 carrots, peeled and roughly chopped

2 large onions, peeled and halved

1 celery stick, roughly chopped

1 Bouquet Garni

$^{1}/_{2}$ tsp salt

4 black peppercorns, lightly crushed

1 Put the carcass and water in a large heavy-based saucepan over a medium-high heat and slowly bring to just below the boil, skimming the surface constantly to remove the grey foam. Do not let the water boil or the stock will be cloudy.

2 When the foam stops forming, add the remaining ingredients and leave the stock to simmer for 2–2$^{1}/_{4}$ hours, skimming the surface occasionally if necessary.

3 Strain the stock and discard the flavouring ingredients. The stock is now ready to use or it can be left to cool completely, then chilled for up to 3 days, as long as it is brought to a full rolling boil before use. Alternatively, it can be frozen for up to 6 months.

*cook's tip

Chicken carcass bones can be frozen to make stock at a convenient time. Put the frozen bones in a large saucepan with water to cover and bring to the boil, then drain the bones, return to the washed pan and follow the recipe above.

vegetable stock

MAKES ABOUT 1.2 LITRES/2 PINTS

2 tbsp sunflower oil

2 large shallots, roughly chopped

1.7 litres/3 pints water

4 celery sticks, roughly chopped

1 carrot, peeled and roughly chopped

selection of vegetable trimmings, such as cabbage leaves, celery leaves, mushroom trimmings, onion skins and tomato skins

1 Bouquet Garni

$^{1}/_{2}$ tsp salt

6 black peppercorns, lightly crushed

1 Heat the oil in a large heavy-based saucepan over a medium-high heat. Add the shallots and sauté for 2-3 minutes until soft, but not coloured.

2 Pour in the water, then add the remaining ingredients and slowly bring to the boil, skimming the surface as necessary. Reduce the heat to very low, partially cover the saucepan and leave the stock to simmer for about 2 hours, skimming the surface if necessary.

3 Strain the stock and discard the flavouring ingredients. The stock is now ready to use or it can be left to cool completely, then chilled for up to 2 days. Alternatively, it can be frozen for up to 6 months.

fish stock

MAKES ABOUT 1.4 LITRES/2 1/2 PINTS

900 g-1.3 kg/2-3 lb fish heads, bones and tails, with any
   large bones cracked and without any gills*

1.2 litres/2 pints water

500 ml/18 fl oz dry white wine

1 onion, thinly sliced

1 leek, halved, rinsed and chopped

1 carrot, peeled and sliced

6 sprigs of fresh flat-leaf parsley

1 bay leaf

4 black peppercorns, lightly crushed

1 Put the fish trimmings, water and wine in a large heavy-based saucepan over a medium-high heat and slowly bring to the boil, skimming the surface constantly to remove the grey foam.

2 When the foam stops forming, reduce the heat to low, add the remaining ingredients and leave the stock to simmer for 30 minutes, skimming the surface occasionally if necessary.

3 Strain the stock and discard the flavouring ingredients. The stock is now ready to use or it can be left to cool completely, then chilled for 1 day, as long as it is brought to a full rolling boil before use. Alternatively, it can be frozen for up to 6 months.

*cook's tip
Do not include any oily fish trimmings as they will make the stock cloudy and their flavours are too strong. Rinse the trimmings to remove any blood before using.

index